Moving
Beyond Loss

Moving Beyond Loss

Real Answers to Real Questions from Real People

Russell Friedman and John W. James

TAYLOR TRADE PUBLISHING
Lanham • New York • Boulder • Toronto • Plymouth, UK

Published by Taylor Trade Publishing
An imprint of The Rowman & Littlefield Publishing Group, Inc.
4501 Forbes Boulevard, Suite 200, Lanham, Maryland 20706
www.rowman.com

10 Thornbury Road, Plymouth PL6 7PP, United Kingdom

Distributed by National Book Network

British Library Cataloguing in Publication Information Available

Library of Congress Cataloging-in-Publication Data

Friedman, Russell.
   Moving beyond loss : real answers to real questions from real
people / Russell Friedman and John W. James.
      p. cm.
   ISBN 978-1-58979-705-5 (pbk. : alk. paper)
   1. Grief. 2. Loss (Psychology) 3. Bereavement—Psychological
aspects. 4. Adjustment (Psychology) I. James, John W. II. Title.
   BF575.G7F738 2013
   155.9'3—dc23

                                                    2012027711

∞™ The paper used in this publication meets the minimum
requirements of American National Standard for Information
Sciences—Permanence of Paper for Printed Library Materials,
ANSI/NISO Z39.48-1992.

Printed in the United States of America

Grieving people do not lack courage or willingness.

What they lack is proper information with which to discover and complete what has been left emotionally unfinished by the death of someone important in their lives.

With this book, we hope to fill in the gap with correct and helpful information that will lead them to the actions of The Grief Recovery Method®, which will help them reclaim a productive place in their lives.

We dedicate this book to the thousands of courageous grievers who have contacted us for help with their broken hearts.

From our hearts to yours,

Russell and John

CONTENTS

PART III   A Host of Questions on
                Unique Situations   **139**

CHAPTER 11   Holidays, Anniversaries, and
                  Reminders: Q&A   141

CHAPTER 12   Stuck on a Painful Image: Q&A   157

INTRODUCTION

We are John W. James and Russell Friedman, founders of The Grief Recovery Institute and creators of The Grief Recovery Method.® Our mission is: "To help the largest amount of grieving people in the shortest time possible." With that mission statement comes a sense of urgency because we know that grieving people need help *now*. We know because when we meet someone who finds out what we do they often ask "Where were you when I needed you fifteen years ago?"

The willingness and ability to help grieving people wasn't a "career choice" that each of us made one day. It's the by-product of the grief we each experienced, coupled with the recovery we gained as the result of painstaking trial and experimentation to learn what would help us deal with our own losses.

It started in 1977 when John's three-day-old son died. As he struggled with the overwhelming impact of his son's death, he realized he had no idea what he could do to help himself. He had to find a way to deal with his broken heart, because he knew he couldn't go on feeling the way he did.

He began his odyssey of discovery by haunting bookstores. All he found were first person books describing pain, but offering no recovery. Not finding a book to help him, John began asking people he thought should know about dealing with grief.

Many of the people he looked to for guidance pointed him at intellectual ideas about life and the meaning of it all, but that didn't help because his heart was broken, not his head. Others aimed him at religious and spiritual philosophies, and even 12-Step programs. They also weren't helpful, because again, it was his heart that was broken and those concepts didn't address his emotions.

In desperation, finding no outside help, John began to work on creating a solution. One of the first things he did was to ask the question, "What is different about the death of my son from the death of my father and the death of my younger brother?" His answer was that even though his father had died at a relatively young age, and his brother, tragically, at twenty, the death of the baby had ended all of the *hopes, dreams, and expectations* John had had for his son and their life together. That one piece of language opened the door for John to realize that the key to recovery was about the relationship he had with his son—no matter how short—and the fact that the hopes and dreams he had could not be realized. From there, John was able to see there were several things he wished had happened differently or better during his wife's pregnancy, and certainly in the events that did and didn't happen in the hospital after his son was born.

John took those ideas and used them to help him review the relationship he had with his son. He realized that in addition to discovering those elements, he was going to have to find a way to complete the discoveries.

With no road map other than his own instinct, and again with a lot of trial and experiment, John pieced together a series of actions that led him to feel emotionally complete with his son. He could still be sad and miss his son, but the pain diminished and that gave him a renewed sense that he could participate in life. By becoming emotionally complete with his son, John did not forget him but rather enabled himself to remember him without pain.

When people found out that John had discovered a unique way to help himself deal with his grief, they started sending others whose baby had died to John for guidance. At that time, John was in the construction business and not really trained to help others. But he couldn't turn those people away. He started spending so much time helping others that the construction business disappeared and The Grief Recovery Institute came into being.

As John's days—and sometimes nights—were taken up helping grieving people one at a time, he realized there were millions of people who needed to know what to do in reaction to their grief. With that, he recognized that he had to write a book, the book he had searched for and never found after his son died. One of John's excellent qualities is that he keeps notes. When he started to write the first edition of *The Grief Recovery Handbook* in 1985, those notes came in very handy.

John self-published *The Grief Recovery Handbook* in 1986. A year later, he sold the publishing rights to HarperCollins (then Harper & Row) and with then partner, Frank Cherry, refined the original book, adding a subtitle, *A Step-by-Step Program for Moving Beyond Loss.*

Russell Friedman arrived at the Institute in 1987, on the heels of a second divorce and a bankruptcy, the combined impact of which brought him to his knees. By that time, John had established the foundation principles and actions of The Grief Recovery Method® in Personal Workshops and Trainings, and in the first two editions of *The Grief Recovery Handbook.*

In 1998, HarperCollins agreed to publish a revised edition of the *Handbook.* John and Russell were able to add divorce and other losses to the content of the book. The new subtitle became, *The Action Program for Moving Beyond Death, Divorce, and Other Losses.* The additions in that version enabled John and

Russell to expand their mission of helping the largest amount of grieving people in the shortest time possible.

Over the twenty-five years that Russell has been a part of the Institute, his mother and father have died, as have several other important people in his life. He has used the principles and actions of grief recovery to help him deal with those deaths as well as other losses that have affected him. Taking care of himself allows him to be able and willing to help others.

This Book Has Been Writing Itself for Thirty-five Years

When John first started helping other grievers, he fielded many questions in person, on the phone, and by mail, and then with the advent of the Internet, via email. Although most of the people who sought John's help in the early days were dealing with the death of a child, soon others called who were dealing with the deaths of spouses, parents, and other important people in their lives. John realized that the actions that helped him and others whose child had died also helped those who were dealing with the death of someone other than a child. Eventually, it became apparent that those actions could also help people deal with divorce and other losses.

In 1988 John and Russell started a national toll-free service called the *Grief Recovery Helpline* which soon was dominating their time and attention. They spent countless hours on the *Helpline* answering the questions posed by grieving people, some of whom were dealing with a very raw, recent loss, others with a loss or losses from long ago. Over the ten years that the *Helpline* existed, John and Russell answered more than 50,000 calls. The results of the experience they gained from the *Helpline* calls are a large part of the answers that appear in this book.

Their second book, *When Children Grieve*, exists in great part because of the thousands of questions they got on the *Helpline*.

Parents and other guardians asked them how to help the children in their care deal with death, divorce, pet loss, moving, and other losses. In writing that book, John and Russell were able to answer what they knew to be the questions of so many people who saw their children struggling but didn't know how to help them.

Even though *The Grief Recovery Handbook* addressed the issue of divorce, there was a demand for a book devoted exclusively to divorce and other romantic relationship endings. Again, responding to the questions they'd heard many times, John and Russell wrote *Moving On: Dump Your Relationship Baggage and Make Room for the Love of Your Life*. Since it only deals with romantic relationship endings, it allows the reader to focus on that arena and accomplish a great deal by taking the actions it outlines. There are several references to divorce in this book and *Moving On* is recommended to those readers struggling with a divorce.

Throughout the years they have constantly delivered emotionally intense three-day Personal Workshops and equally powerful four-and-a-half-day Grief Recovery Method® Certification training programs.

John and Russell Talk about Their Collaboration with Tributes.com

In 2010, Tributes.com invited us to provide Grief Recovery Method® guidance on their website. Tributes.com, which receives more than a million and a half unique visitors each month, is the online resource for current local and national obituary news, and an online community to provide support during times of loss and grieving.

Our original commitment to Tributes.com was to provide helpful articles on the topic of grief recovery, and to initiate an *Ask The Experts* section for grieving people. We invited visitors to that site to email us with their specific questions as they tried to deal with the aftermath of the death of someone important in their lives.

We were thrilled to have that forum, and we're grateful to Tributes.com for the faith and trust they placed in us. We knew that our articles would be valuable to all of their visitors. What we didn't know was that the *Ask The Experts* section was going to lead to this book. This book is an edited compilation of many of the questions we've received and the answers we've given over the years, not just those that were published on Tributes.com. Although we answered every Tributes.com question, we only published those we believe a great deal of people can relate to and will benefit from.

In the beginning, questions trickled in at the rate of three or four a week. We took the time to read each one carefully and respond personally to the specific questions and concerns they contained. After the first few weeks, we had created a signature line that said, "From our hearts to yours, Russell and John."

The *Ask The Experts* feature quickly became very popular and the volume of questions went from three or four a week to between ten and twenty, and sometimes more, where it has remained ever since. As the questions poured in from real grievers, we realized they were different than the standard kinds of questions you might see listed as *frequently asked* by grieving people. They were raw and gritty, and detailed with the very personal things those new grievers were experiencing. The questions were poignant and profound. We felt compelled to give the best guidance we could to each person.

The *Ask The Experts* feature was a perfect way for us to continue to honor our mission of "helping the largest amount of grieving people in the shortest time possible." It also represented a way for us to be "in the trenches" with grieving people, but only at their request. We didn't intervene, as strangers, in their worlds. We let them come to us to ask for guidance.

The invitation to send questions to Tributes.com allowed people to write anonymously and permitted us to publish their questions and our replies with their first names. We asked for permission to reprint their questions and our responses so that many more people could be helped. Even though we have their permission, we've chosen to change all the names and locations to give those people absolute confidentiality.

Adapting the Questions and Answers to Book Form

Since the objective of our answers is always to direct people to real help, nearly every response contains the direction, "Go to the library or bookstore and get a copy of *The Grief Recovery Handbook*," or in some cases, *When Children Grieve*. To avoid repetition, in preparing this book for publication, we modified our answers so you won't have to read that direction about getting the books every time. In its place, you'll see phrases like, "As you take the actions of grief recovery . . ." or "As you read and take the actions outlined in the *Handbook* . . ."

Also, in our answers to questions on Tributes.com, we occasionally refer grieving people to online links to articles we have previously written. We've reprinted those articles in the back of this book to make it easier for you to access them.

This book is split into three main sections, beginning with questions which relate to the Six Myths of Grief; followed by a section contrasting the alleged Stages of Grief with Typical, Normal, and Natural Responses to Loss; and a third section on a variety of questions from unique situations that don't fall under a convenient section heading. After the series of questions and answers, you'll find reprints of the articles that are referenced in several of our responses.

Small and Correct Choices

When someone important to us dies, we automatically review that relationship and discover things we wish had been *different, better, or more,* and we lament the unrealized *hopes, dreams, and expectations* we had for the future. You may or may not be consciously aware of that review, but we assure you that it happens.

Recovery from the impact of the death of someone important to us is achieved by a series of small and correct actions. Sadly, many people don't know that recovery is even possible, nor do they know what those actions are. Grieving people are courageous and willing, but without correct information about those actions, and absent a safe environment in which to take them, they tend to bury their grief inside where it can only get worse.

The primary purposes of this book are to give you hope that recovery is possible for you or someone you care about, and to introduce you to The Grief Recovery Method.®

Whether you're reading this book for yourself, or on behalf of someone you care about, it will give you a wealth of new awareness about grief and unresolved grief. It's not designed to spell out the specific actions of The Grief Recovery Method.® For that we'll direct you to *The Grief Recovery Handbook, When Children Grieve,* and *Moving On.* Those books demonstrate and explain grief recovery actions in detail, giving you a road map to overcoming the pain caused by loss. They are available at www .griefrecoverymethod.com and at most bookstores and libraries.

The real answers to the real questions in this book are the product of years of applying the principles and actions of The Grief Recovery Method® to the nonstop questions we've received from those grieving people who are courageous enough to ask.

From our hearts to yours,
Russell and John

PART ONE

Beginning at the Beginning

Nowhere in life are our emotions more affected by what we believe than in our responses to grief. In the introduction we said, "Grief is the normal and natural reaction to loss, but almost everything we learn about dealing with grief is not normal, not natural, and not helpful." In order for this book to make sense to you, it's important that you understand what we mean by that.

What we think and believe about everything we perceive dictates how we feel. That may seem like an odd statement, since many people think their feelings come first. But that's not true. In order for you to have feelings about anything, you must first put a value on whatever has happened that might affect you emotionally. The value you put on something, whether you believe it to be good or bad, or right or wrong, comes from your personal belief system.

Over the thirty-five years we've been helping grieving people, we've identified six major myths about grief that are so close to universal that nearly everyone can relate to them.

That's true not only for those of us raised and socialized here in America, but for people from different cultures speaking different languages around the world.

As an example, we remember a woman who called us several years ago and said, "My mother died a year ago and I haven't cried yet! Is there something wrong with me?" It may surprise you to learn that our first response was to ask her, "Do you normally cry when something sad happens?" But it was no surprise to us when she said "NO!" quite emphatically, followed by, "As a little girl growing up in Switzerland, we would get in trouble if we cried—we were always told we had to 'be strong.'"

You might already have guessed that the idea of "being strong" (and "being strong for others") is one of the six myths that we're going to detail in the opening chapters.

Chapter One of this section gives a short-form explanation for these myths, each of which tends to negatively impact what would be our normal and natural reactions to loss—in particular the death of someone who was meaningful in our lives. Chapters Two through Five feature the myths presented in the context of real questions from grieving people and our responses. The section on myths will provide you with a foundation for understanding our responses to grievers' questions in Parts Two and Three.

CHAPTER ONE

SIX MYTHS THAT LIMIT US

A great deal of the information and misinformation we learn in childhood stays with us for the rest of our lives. Nowhere is this more evident—and more unhelpful— than in the area of grief and what to do about it. Because so many of the questions you read in this book are based on the six myths, we want you to be familiar with them.

Here are the six myths as they appear in *The Grief Recovery Handbook, When Children Grieve,* and *Moving On*:

- Don't Feel Bad
- Replace the Loss
- Grieve Alone
- Grief Just Takes Time or Time Heals All Wounds
- Be Strong & Be Strong for Others
- Keep Busy

When these myths are exposed, most people realize they've been influenced by them all their lives but have never taken a critical look at them to see if they're accurate or helpful. While our parents and others may have inadvertently passed on life-limiting rather than life-enhancing information to us on the topic of grief and what to do about it, we know there was no intent to harm us—they were passing on what had been handed down to them.

Let us give you an example based on the fact that a huge percentage of the thousands of questions we get every year are focused on the myth "time heals all wounds." Just this morning, an email came in with this question: "My dad died in August, 2007. I was Daddy's girl and my life revolved around him. Everyone says time heals . . . it hasn't. It feels as if it happened yesterday. I'm hurting just as much today as I did the day I lost him. When will this pain end?"

The young woman who sent that question was socialized in the same world as the rest of us, one which continues to pass on misleading information as if it were fact and which can negatively affect the rest of our lives. When we take in an idea like "time heals all wounds" in childhood, we believe it and carry it forward as truth, because it usually comes to us from a high authority source—our parents, teachers, clergy, and others in positions of authority. After a major grief event affects our lives, and we're confronted with the reality that time doesn't heal our emotional wounds, we become trapped. Part of the trap is thinking that we're defective because we're not healing within time as we should. Another part is that the false belief that time will heal us stops us from looking for and taking actions that might actually help. In effect, the belief that time heals paralyzes us into nonaction. A year or two later we report that it's gotten worse.

To repeat: When we say we were all misinformed about grief, we're not saying that to attack our parents, our schools, our religions, or anything or anybody else. We know our parents got it from their parents, and they from theirs, and that the misinformation about dealing with grief is being passed down from generation to generation, without anyone stopping to ask, "Is this true?" or "Is this valid?"

It's unlikely you asked those questions when you were young. As you read about the myths, we want you to ask them now, even of yourself.

Myth #1—Don't Feel Bad!

Even though grief and all of the feelings associated with it are normal and natural, children are constantly told not to feel the way they feel. This automatically puts them in conflict with the truth, in conflict with their own nature, and indeed, in conflict with the parents and guardians who are supposed to help them.

To illustrate, we use the story of a child who comes home from preschool with tears in her eyes. Her mom or dad asks, "What happened?" and the child responds truthfully, "The other little girls were mean to me." To which the parent says, *"Don't feel bad,* here have a cookie, you'll feel better." In reality, the cookie doesn't make the child feel better—it makes her feel different. She has merely been distracted from her hurt feelings. She has been told by her parents, whom she trusts, not to feel bad, even though she does. She has also been taught that when she feels bad she should medicate herself with a substance, in this case, sugar.

In addition, she's taking in the idea that feeling bad or sad is bad rather than being a normal emotional reaction to a loss, no matter how small or large it may seem. From that point forward, the little girl is liable to start *not* telling the truth to her parents (and others) and begin burying her sad or painful feelings.

If the child had come home happy with a wonderful report about her day, her parents would *not* have said, "Don't feel good!" This silly example hammers home the idea that it's only the sad, painful, or negative feelings that we're told not to feel, and that we should cover those feelings up with substances. This early teaching becomes the default for how we think about our feelings throughout the rest of our lives, and whether or not we express them openly.

We want you to start thinking about this for yourself, as a person who has and may again feel the pain of grief. Or, if you're reading this book because you're concerned about someone you love who's dealing with grief, we want you to be able to help them in some way, if only by *not* saying, "Don't feel bad." They have every reason in the world to feel bad or sad if someone important to them has died.

Sadness and fear are the most typical emotional reactions attached to loss of any kind. They are essential to being human. They must have equality of expression along with happy feelings. This must start in childhood and continue throughout our lives.

Myth #2—Replace the Loss

Children hear "replace the loss" as the second section of a phrase everyone knows—"Don't feel bad; on Saturday we'll get you a new dog." In reality, while we can get another dog, the irreplaceable element is the relationship with the dog that died.

Sadly the concept of replacing the loss continues in full force in areas other than death. When a teenager's first romantic fling ends, she or he is likely to be told, "Don't feel bad, there are plenty of fish in the sea." Freely translated, "replace the loss" equals "just go get another boyfriend or girlfriend."

Most of the time when your mother or father dies, you won't hear, "Don't feel bad. You can get another mother," but we can't tell you how many widows and widowers have told us that well-meaning friends said, "Don't feel bad. You're young; you can remarry."

One of the most painful pieces of advice we've ever heard was given to John twenty minutes after his son died, "Don't feel sad. You should feel grateful; you and your wife can have other children." That comment mixes the first two myths—"Don't Feel Bad" and "Replace the Loss"—into one emotionally lethal combination. Even though the person who said it intended it to be helpful and comforting, it was not.

The essential fact remains that you cannot replace relationships, so you must first grieve and complete your relationship with the person who died, whether you ever wish to remarry, have other children, or expand your relationships with new people.

Myth #3—Grieve Alone

This all-encompassing myth shackles adults and children alike. Almost everyone has been exposed to this dangerous saying: "Laugh and the whole world laughs with you, cry and you cry alone."

There are many other comments heard in childhood, which contribute to the myth of grieving alone. "If you're going to cry, go to your room" is one of those statements which is made for different purposes, but still creates the effect of establishing that sad feelings are not to be displayed openly.

You may have heard it said that grieving people tend to isolate. That's true, but it's based on many false ideas, one of which is, "You wouldn't want to burden others with your feelings." The most profound truth is that when you get good news you want to share it with the people in your life. The same is true when you get bad news; the first instinct is to call someone. Communicating the truth about how you feel is one of the healthiest things you can do for yourself.

We encourage everyone to be better listeners—not to judge or criticize the feelings our family and friends communicate, especially about their reactions to the death of someone important to them.

Myth #4—Grief Just Takes Time

Sometimes stated as "grief just takes time" or "time heals all wounds," this myth is probably the most frequently heard. Although this topic is not a funny one, we like to illustrate this myth with a humorous example.

If you went to your car and discovered it had a flat tire, would you pull up a chair, sit down, and wait for air to jump back in your tire? Clearly not. You would take the action of changing the tire or calling the auto club for help.

A broken heart can feel like a flat tire—flat and listless—and time can't mend a broken heart any more than it can put air back into a flat tire. Just as you must take actions to repair the flat tire, actions must also be taken to help mend the broken heart.

Although completion and recovery from loss happen *within* time, they are not a function of time. They are accomplished by taking correct grief recovery actions within time. It's essential to learn what those actions are. They are spelled out in detail in *The Grief Recovery Handbook*, which is available at most libraries and bookstores.

Myth #5—Be Strong & Be Strong for Others

Being strong is a myth you definitely should investigate and reverse. As children we copy the behaviors demonstrated by our parents and other adults. It's all too common when a parent, in a misguided attempt to "be strong for the children," displays no emotion at all about a major loss of their own. Perhaps their own parent has died. Instead of showing how they feel, they clam up, but expect, and sometimes even try to force, the child to talk about the feelings the child has about the death. What they don't realize is that they are inadvertently passing on to their children the myth of "being strong" or "being strong for others." The fact is that you can't really "be" anything for someone else. All you can be is honest, which is really the most helpful thing you can do.

Myth #6—Keep Busy

"Keep busy" is one of those instructions grieving people get from well-meaning family and friends following the death of someone important to them. "Keeping busy" is actually a sub-myth based on the faulty idea that "time heals all wounds." Therefore, the idea of keeping busy is: If you can distract yourself in a whirlwind of activity, another day will have passed since the loss, and time can do its job.

Over the years we've seen people who've taken "keep busy" to the point of physical and emotional exhaustion. When that happens they lose sight of the grief they may be pushing down in an attempt to distract themselves.

Equipped with Better Information, You Can Now Decide What to Keep and What to Discard

As you think about the myths we've presented, you might recall some other things you heard growing up. Take a good look at the myths we've outlined and those things from your early life. Think about them and decide if they are valuable for you or if you need to discard them and replace them with more helpful ideas and actions.

The fact that we've been carrying information with us since we were very young doesn't mean that it's accurate. Grievers are most limited by what they think is true. We hope our short explanations about the myths related to grief encourage you to find out more about what is correct and helpful for you.

Also, knowing a little bit about the six myths, you're now better equipped to absorb the lessons in the questions and answers that follow. The first two myths, "Don't Feel Bad" and "Replace the Loss" are themes that run throughout the entire collection of letters, so they do not have their own separate section in the book. We'll begin the letters with the third and one of the most common myths "Grieve Alone."

CHAPTER
TWO

MYTH: GRIEVE ALONE: Q&A

My Husband Never Comes Out of the Bedroom

Sandy from MD writes:
Our twenty-year-old son died last year and it's been a devastating time,
but my husband has closed himself off from us. He never comes out of
the bedroom and seems to be so angry with everything that it's hard to
even live with him. Is this normal and will he ever snap out of this? We
have other kids and they need him to be a part of their life too.

Dear Sandy,

We can only imagine how difficult it is for you and your kids to
have to tiptoe around your husband and his anger and isolation.

You ask if what he's doing is normal. The answer is that it's
all too common and is somewhat within the range of normal
reactions to diabolical situations. Dealing with the death of
anyone, and in particular the death of a child, some people stay
stuck, stay angry, stay away from everyone, and can't seem to
come back out. It's very hard to help them, because they don't
ask for help, and usually don't react well if you offer to help or
suggest that they get some help. If someone doesn't want help,
there's not much you can do.

The best we can suggest is for you and your kids to take care
of yourselves. Hopefully you are each doing things to help you
become emotionally complete with your son—their brother—
who died.

If you feel you need more guidance for yourselves, go to the
library or bookstore and get a copy of *The Grief Recovery Handbook*. As you read it and take the actions it outlines, you may find
yourself better able to interact with your husband. As a result of
what you do for yourself, he may be encouraged to pick up the
book and start reading it. That would be the best possible hope
for him to come out of his shell.

From our hearts to yours,
Russell and John

I Wonder Why I Have to Be All By Myself

Sylvia from VT writes:
My grandma died about three years ago and life completely changed for me. I lost her when I was fifteen years old and never really got along with any of my other family members. If I'd get in a fight with my mom, my grandma would be there for me. She died really suddenly and I'm still consumed with grief. I feel like there's no point in the future because I planned my ENTIRE future around her. There are so many moments when I wonder why I have to be all by myself. My grandpa is still alive but I find myself pulling away from him and the family as a whole. I was just wondering, is life ever going to pan out and will I get to a point where I feel it's okay that she died and I'm alone?

Dear Sylvia,

We imagine that it was overwhelming for you when your grandma died, the person who was probably the safest person in your life—the one you could always trust. We certainly understand what you mean when you say that your vision of the future always included her in your life, at least for many more years. We also know that it's normal and natural for grieving people to pull away from family and friends, usually out of a sense of wanting to protect themselves from further hurt, if one of them should die. The problem with that is that by pulling away, more hurt is created, and if they die, you have a double dose of the pain of their death along with the awareness that you had pulled away from them.

Taking grief recovery method actions will help you feel more emotionally complete with the physical absence of your grandma; help you rebuild new dreams for the future; and help you make a choice to move toward rather than away from your grandpa and others.

One of the things we hope for you is that a partial result of taking the actions will be that you can have fond memories of your grandma that will not turn painful for you. Even though the dreams you had for life included her being there with you, you'll be able to share her from your heart with the people who are part of your life.

From our hearts to yours,
Russell and John

Her Emotional Plate Is Way Beyond Full

Flora from NM writes:
I never had a person die close to me until five years ago—my ex over-
dosed at twenty-eight. A year later there were more including my
mother who died the day I scheduled a flight to introduce her to her
new granddaughter. After that was the suicide of a close friend, cancer
of a schoolmate, and then my father was sick for several months and
died last year. I feel so numb and distant, antisocial is an understate-
ment. I frequent cemeteries and sit at graves of old friends. I read
obituaries daily, don't want to talk to anyone about this, I just don't
feel like they are "with me." Now my sisters are finally falling apart
and not only can I not help myself, I can't possibly help them either. I
have a religious upbringing that believes there is no afterlife, so I am
really lost on many levels.

Dear Flora,

Wow, your emotional plate is way beyond full!

Let's start by telling you that "numb" is the most typical response grievers feel in reaction to the death of someone. It is the
most normal and natural reaction.

When you say you are feeling "distant and antisocial," our
response is to say that "grieving people tend to isolate" for a variety of reasons. Again, what you're experiencing is well within
the range of normal and natural.

As to your feeling that no one is "with" you: we hear you
loud and clear. We know that most people don't know how to
either listen to or talk to grievers, so while that's accurate, it
doesn't make you feel any better—in fact it is probably one of
the elements that leads to the feeling of being "distant and antisocial." A problem within that is that it's not your job to educate
the people around you about how to listen and talk.

And of course you can't help your sisters, in part because
you don't know how to help yourself. Hopefully, if you follow

the guidance we give you here, your sisters will see some positive changes in you, and will want to know what you did.

We want to acknowledge your comment about your beliefs about an afterlife. Again we hear you, and we're pretty sure we know what you mean. We really believe that grief recovery actions will help you become emotionally complete with all the major people from your life who have died, so that you can take care of yourself in real time, here on earth, and not even have to be concerned about any future ideas in a different realm at this point.

As you take the actions, you'll sense positive shifts in how you think and feel. Since you have a host of losses due to death—and possibly other non-death related losses—you'll have to invest some time and energy into this work. We know it will sometimes be difficult to find the energy because unresolved grief drains energy, but the good news is that as you take the actions, you will find your energy coming back.

From our hearts to yours,
Russell and John

It's Not Advisable for Family Members to Do Grief Work Together

Linda from CT writes:
My family is so dysfunctional that I find myself grieving alone. How can I do this? Any ideas?

Dear Linda,
There's no doubt that isolation is one of the biggest issues grievers have to face, both in general society, and sadly, within their own families. We're sure it's painful for you not to be able to grieve with your family members (assuming they also suffer from the loss). Our book *The Grief Recovery Handbook* will help you take the actions that will help you deal with your own grief, with or without the support of your family.

The actions in the book are intended to be done in partnership with another griever who would be working on his or her own loss, but it's not advisable for family members to work together when they're dealing with the death of the same person. So from that point of view, your "dysfunctional" family won't prevent you from taking actions that can help you recover from the loss, because you'd never be working in partnership with any of them.

The book also lays out a plan for those people who have no one to work with or who, for whatever reasons, are unwilling to partner up with someone.

From our hearts to yours,
Russell and John

"Let Go" of What? and "Move On" to Where?

Bryan from VA writes:
I am a Vietnam veteran. Several close friends of mine were killed in action. They ranged in age from 19 to 20 years old. These young soldiers were great friends. One moment they were there, and the next they were gone. This still weighs heavily on my heart and I can't seem to "let it go." Do you have any suggestions?

Dear Bryan,

I'm going to give you some general guidance in response to your questions about "letting go," and then I'm going to share a response from John W. James, our founder, who is also a Vietnam vet. His experience probably parallels yours to a great degree. He'll give you some specifics that relate to that experience.

One of the cliché phrases that has crept into our language is, "You have to let go and move on." Our response to that is "Let go of what?" "Move on to where?" and "How do I do that?" Those are pretty much the same questions we've gotten from grieving people over the years who've been given that strange piece of advice. You wouldn't want to let go of fond memories—you'd probably want to keep them. You'd probably not like to be limited by painful memories, but how do you make that happen? The bottom line is that you would move on from the pain that weighs heavily on your heart, if only you knew how to do that.

We hope you'll take the actions outlined in *The Grief Recovery Handbook*. They will guide you in discovering and completing what was left emotionally unfinished for you in your relationships with your friends who died. As you take the actions, you'll find a reduction in that sense of a heavy heart and, with that, a new ability to move forward in your life without forgetting those people you lost.

John adds: *Society and their own early childhood training often isolate grievers. This is even truer for veterans who are in a very small and select group within the general population. Less than 1 percent of all US citizens ever serves in the military or experiences the type of losses you describe. We've had countless veterans in our programs over the years and in every case the issue of unfinished emotional business is a major one. What is common in the military experience is that close relationships are developed based on unusual circumstances.*

It's probably true that you trusted these several friends more than some of the members of your own family. You trusted them to protect you when you slept and you returned that trust by protecting them. Most of the time these trusts are never discussed. And when one of those people we trusted dies, we feel cheated out of the chance to tell them our truth. The truth would be in the form of having a way to tell them exactly how you felt about them and another major part would be to say the "goodbyes" that you didn't get a chance to say.

From our hearts to yours,
Russell and John

I'm Scared, but Will Do It Anyway

Anonymous from CA writes:
The man I lived with for twenty years died suddenly and unexpectedly
last fall. We were apart only two weeks during our entire relationship. I
cannot process the kind of pain and deep loss I am feeling. To complicate
matters, he was an obsessive controller. He shopped, did laundry, and
I wasn't even allowed to get the mail or see a bill. It's been five months
and I'm not able to function. I lie to my friends and say I paid my bills
and my mailbox is full. I'm not lazy. I try, but there's this invisible
source that stops me. Will this ever go away?

Dear Anon,
As strange as it may seem to you, your lament is not that unusual. We've heard it many times.

Our definition of grief is, "The conflicting feelings caused
by an end or change in familiar pattern of behavior." For twenty
years, what you were "familiar" with was him doing everything.
Now that he's gone, it's almost as if you're paralyzed and can't
do anything. It makes sense to us that the "invisible source" that
stops you is the *habit and memory* of the past twenty years. That
habit and memory put you so much in mind of him and how
much you miss him, that you stop yourself. The key here is in
recognizing that the emotions involved in him being physically
absent from your life—while powerful and valid—cannot stop
you from taking care of the day-to-day actions of your life.

Here's a little something you can use to help yourself. Decide
that you must go to the mailbox and say to yourself, "My heart is
broken, I miss him so much, AND, I need to go out to the mailbox and take care of important things in my life. I'm scared, and
I don't want to do it, but I will do it anyway."

Doing it that way, you can have the fear and other feelings,
but still take the actions you need to take. Then, sometime after
you've gotten the mail, you can sit down at the table and say, "My

heart is broken, I miss him so much, AND, I need to pay these bills and take care of my life. I'm scared, and I don't want to do it, but I will do it anyway."

Using this idea, one thing at a time, you can start to take care of yourself while still honoring your feelings of sadness, loneliness, etc.

From our hearts to yours,
Russell and John

MYTH: IT JUST TAKES TIME: Q&A

The Pain Often Gets Worse within Time

Leslie from NH writes:

My dad died a year ago. Ever since, it's been daily grief for me. A few weeks after Dad, two of my uncles died. I've always been so close to my parents, I feel as if I lost a part of me when Dad died. I worry about my Mom. I make sure she's okay and that she's eating and has someone to talk to, but it's so hard trying to talk to her while I'm going through my grief too. I feel selfish and don't know how to feel or what to say. I don't like life anymore and don't want to do anything really. I feel forced into a lot. Is this normal? People say in time the pain gets lighter, but so far it's only gotten worse.

Dear Leslie,

One of the sad truths in your note is a comment we hear regularly from grieving people; time not only doesn't heal emotional wounds but with the passage of time, the pain often feels worse.

In our books and lectures, we constantly talk about the *six myths of grief*, one of which is that "time heals all wounds." The best example we can give of how time *doesn't* fix anything is the image of a flat tire. If you just pull up a chair and sit and stare at a flat tire, you can sit there for a thousand years and that tire is going to stay flat.

You must take actions to repair the flat tire or you're not going to get back on the road. One action is to get out the jack and the spare tire, and change the tire yourself. The other is to realize the main reason you have a cell phone, and call the auto club to come and change the tire. Either way, action must be taken so you can drive again.

The parallel is that a broken heart is remarkably like a flat tire. The energy for life is limited. And as you say, "I don't like life anymore and don't want to do anything really. I feel forced into a lot." Those are powerful words, and indicate the level and degree to which your emotional tires are flat.

The answer to your question, "Is this normal?" is YES! Having your own grief and trying to help someone else at the same time is awkward and difficult at best. Your thought that you might be selfish is honorable, but not accurate. You're trying to deal with your own broken heart, which is a full-time job. The fact that you love and care about your mom is obvious from your other comments.

We also want to comment on your powerful statement, *"I've always been so close to my parents, I feel as if I lost a part of me when Dad died."* That sentiment is one that we hear all the time, and we know that it's a very normal feeling that represents the physical feelings we have when someone very important to us dies.

As you take grief recovery actions, the energy and desire to participate in life will return for you, and will allow you to be more present and available to your Mom, if you choose to do that.

From our hearts to yours,
Russell and John

Do We Ever Really Recover?

Sally from HI writes:
Do we ever really "recover?" It is almost four years since I lost my hus-
band to liver disease. The holidays are still difficult to bear. He would
have just had a birthday and I did not have a good day. Also, he died on
my birthday and I can't celebrate anymore. Don't we just deal with it
rather than recover from it?

Dear Sally,
Great question. Many people question the idea of recovery from
loss because they never forget the person who died—which
makes sense, because until or unless you ever get Alzheimer's,
you're not going to forget someone who was important to you.
Most importantly, you would never want to forget your husband
and in so doing lose the fond memories of your life together.

The key to recovery is to discover and complete what was
left emotionally unfinished at the time of the death. Almost
always, when someone important to us dies, we discover things
we wish had happened *differently, better, or more,* and find we're
left with unrealized *hopes, dreams, and expectations* for the future.

The other recovery related issue is part of what you said, in
that it has been almost four years since your husband died. One
of the biggest myths in the world is that "time heals all wounds."
The truth is that it takes actions to deal with a broken heart.

And yes, the major holidays, as well as birthdays—yours and
his—and Valentine's Day, can all become fearful, sad, and painful
reminders that he's no longer here.

As to the idea of "just dealing with it": We've known of so
many people who've tried to do that. Many people in attempting
to "just deal with it" try to bypass and bury the pain, but that just
doesn't work. Your own story seems to be a case in point.

Let's face it, even without knowing any more about you than
is in your short note, we can guess that your relationship with

your husband was positive and life affirming for you, and his absence is incredibly difficult. How would you be able to "just deal with it?" It wouldn't make sense.

You must take actions to deal with your grief to become emotionally complete so that you can have fond memories that do not turn painful, and so that you are able to participate in holidays and have emotions on birthdays without pain. You may have normal and natural sadness and miss him on those days—as you do on other days—but the pain will go away.

From our hearts to yours,
Russell and John

They Want Us Looking Good and Being Productive 3–5 Days Later!

Caitlin from MO writes:
I keep asking myself, "Why me?" I lost my son in November, my dad in January, and now, my oldest daughter. Everyone wants to know why I'm so weepy! I have one daughter left (and three grandchildren) and I panic if I don't hear from her a couple of times a day. I need peace. Apparently I'm a beast they think should be heavily medicated, but my mind overrules that. Thanks for listening.

Hi Caitlin,
When we read a note like yours, with loss after loss after loss, we always think of someone drowning in the ocean. Every time their head starts to come above the surface, another wave comes and pushes them under.

"Why me?" is a pretty logical question in those circumstances, even though there is no real answer for it. We'd guess you're weepy because your heart is broken. We're surprised—and saddened—that the people around you don't get that. But remember, we live in a strange world that wants us back at our desk at work, 3–5 days after the death of someone important in our lives.

And they want us to look good, feel good, and be productive. And of course, when you're grieving, which usually includes crying and not necessarily being at the top of your game, they want to medicate you.

We're thrilled that you are ruling out the drugs because, for the most part, all they do is cover up the pain; they don't make it go away. In the meantime, it gets worse inside of you. We're on your side; however, as you've probably figured out, time on its own won't heal your broken heart, but taking grief recovery actions can help.

From our hearts to yours,
Russell and John

Answering Questions Doesn't Resolve Grief

Maryanne from OH writes:
My husband of twenty-five years died two years ago from cancer. He didn't even know he had it until he had to go to the hospital and he died four days later. He only knew for four days that he even had this. I was in another state with another family emergency and this happened—no one even called me til the day AFTER he died and left a voice mail at that. When I got there I was told I had come for no reason and to go home. I wasn't allowed to see him before he was cremated. I was told if I showed up at the funeral and burial of his ashes, I would be arrested. I wasn't even mentioned in the obituary.

Now he's gone and I'm so alone. I feel like I have a hole in my chest the size of the universe. As I sit here and type this I can't even do it without crying. I cry all the time, it hurts so bad. We never went a day in twenty-five years without talking on the phone, e-mailing, or being with each other in person. When he was out of town, each day he would tell me how much he loved and missed me. Now, there's NOTHING. On top of this, his family won't talk to me so I don't know if anyone was with him when he died, or if he died alone; if he suffered or not. These are things I need to know and I don't know where to get the answers.

My brother & mom tell me I need to just move on and "suck it up," that they understand why I feel this way, but that I can't live the rest of my life like this. I want to be with him so badly. He's been my everyday living, breathing life and soul for so many years. I'm just so lost and half of me is with him. How can I live now that he's dead?

Dear Maryanne,
What a devastating situation to be in. While we can't tell you how to find the answers you seek to questions about your husband's death, one thing we recommend is that you get some guidance for dealing with your grief, even while you're looking for those answers.

As to the grief of "not knowing," we're aware how awful it is for people to not have information about the death of people who are meaningful to them. We know that in their search to find out what happened, they often overlook the need to work on the grief of the death itself, rather than the cause of the death. When people are focused on how and why a death occurred, they really tend to get stuck in the pain. If and when they do find out what happened, their hearts are no better than before they found out. That's all the more reason to start working on your grief right away.

The image of only being partially here is powerful, but is dangerous for setting up the idea that life is not valuable without him. Since he was such a wonderful man, one thing that will help you is to share this goodness of him with others—focusing more on the presence he had in your life rather than on his death and absence.

A personal note from Russell: Something that helps me is the idea that I am the continuation of my mother and father, who are both dead, and that to a certain degree, I carry forward in my current marriage some of the virtues and goodness of my two previous marriages. Even though each of those endings was painful, I focus on carrying forward the sweetness of each relationship, along with any occasional feelings of "missing" them, which are a natural part of being human.

You were a whole and complete person when you met your husband and his presence in your life allowed you to expand who and what you are. Yes, your life contracts without him here, but you are still a whole and complete person. We hope that you will consider taking grief recovery actions to help you get to a place where you can focus on the entire relationship, not just the ending, and be able to share your memory of him with others.

From our hearts to yours,
Russell and John

How Long until I'm Happy Again?

Anonymous from UT writes:
I'm a freshman in college and my grandfather recently died. I was just wondering how long it will be until I feel like the old happy me I was before he died? I feel lost without him here. He was a part of my life for 19 years and today was so tough because it was my first Easter without talking to him on the phone. I'm wondering how long it takes to get over your grandfather's death?

Dear Anon,

We were very much affected by your sweet, sad question, *"How long it will be until I feel like the old happy me I was before he died?"*

We've all been incorrectly taught or influenced to believe that time heals all wounds. But since time can't heal an emotional wound, the question isn't about time healing, *it's about adapting to a new, painful, and unwanted reality.* As you adapt, however, it doesn't necessarily mean that your broken heart has healed.

One of the things we suggest you do as you are learning to live your life with this major change is to establish at least one person who is safe for you to talk to about how you feel. That way, at any given moment, in person, or by text or email, you could say, "I'm having a really sad moment, missing my grandfather." Having a safe place to tell the truth, you will be able to adapt more quickly and effectively to this reality and to keep fond memories of your relationship with your grandfather.

But just talking about how you feel is not enough. We strongly suggest that you take the actions of grief recovery. When you do that, even though you won't be able to feel exactly the way you did when he was alive, you will be able to remember, talk about, and carry forward the joy you associate with him and with the relationship you shared.

From our hearts to yours,
Russell and John

If You Move On, Are You Letting Go of Them?

Ben from OK writes:

Last year my best friend and another friend were walking down the road when a driver crossed into the opposite lane and onto the shoulder of the road where they were walking, hitting and killing them both. My friends were sixteen and eighteen. The driver was also eighteen. I've not been the same since. I'm only sixteen and I find myself losing much ambition for life. I never seem to be happy. My best friend is always on my mind. When I say I'm losing ambition for life I don't mean I'm suicidal, I just don't get out of the house as much anymore and I've lost interest in hanging out with other friends.

My question would be how to end this constant depression, or at least just ease the pain? I know my best friend would want me to enjoy life, as I did with him. It's just so difficult and I feel awful that I can't. I'm still very close with his family, and have gotten much closer with my other friend's family.

I spend a lot of time up at the cemetery, where they are buried side-by-side. Is it good to go there so often? When I visit them I do seem to be in a better mood. Is it common to feel that if you move on you're letting go of them? How, if possible, do I change that feeling? What about forgiving the driver? I haven't done that, nor do I think I ever will. If you could give me some answers to my questions it would mean a lot. At school people ask me if I'm all right because I look sad, even though I try to pretend I'm ok. I can tell my parents are also concerned about me. I just want to be happier because I know that's what my friends and family would want.

Dear Ben,

That's a painful story to read. We were very much affected by several of the things you said. Frankly, it's almost impossible to imagine what it's like for you to have to carry such a loss around with you. We know that your experience of diminished ambition and reduced happiness is a normal and natural reaction and is typical for grieving people. Knowing that won't change how you feel, but it may help you to know that there's nothing wrong with you for feeling that way.

We want to talk a little about your comment "I've lost interest in hanging out with other friends." That doesn't surprise us. With the experience of the death of your friends, you automatically might withdraw from other friends out of the fear of losing them too. This is especially true when we don't know how to deal with the pain we have from losing someone important to us, and we add the fear of losing other people also. So we pull away rather than moving towards others. It's almost logical even though it really doesn't help. We noticed that you said that you've gotten closer with your other friend's family, and we imagine that's good for all concerned.

You asked about going to the cemetery too often. No one can tell you how often you should visit the gravesite and the fact that your visits seem to help your mood indicates that it's valuable for you.

Next we want to address your questions about letting go and moving on. "Is it common to feel that if you move on you're letting go of them? How, if possible, do I change that feeling?" In order to answer, we want to give you some different language. Letting go implies forgetting, and you will never forget your friends. You don't want to let go. What you want to do is discover and complete what is left emotionally unfinished for you in your relationships with your friends who died. A huge part of what's unfinished for you—in addition to wishing the tragedy hadn't happened—are all the hopes and expectations you had for your future with them that now cannot happen. The other piece of language that might help you shift is instead of thinking of it as "moving on," which may imply you're letting go of them, you might say that as a result of feeling more emotionally complete you will be able to "move forward" in your life. The difference between "moving on" and "moving forward in your life" may be subtle, but it carries different connotations and may help you.

The key for you is to take grief recovery actions which will allow you to remember your friends the way you knew them in life, not only in death; for those memories not to turn painful for you; and for you to be able to have a life of meaning and value even though your friends are gone.

Regarding your question, "What about forgiving the driver?": The topic of forgiveness is one that many grieving people struggle with. We talk about it in all of our books. Please read pages 138–140 in *The Grief Recovery Handbook* to get a better understanding of what forgiveness is and how to go about it. We can tell you if you don't forgive, you'll hold onto the pain you associate with your friends' deaths. The purpose of forgiveness is to free yourself from carrying painful feelings forward; it is not about condoning what other people have done.

Finally—we're concerned about two things you said in your last paragraph: ". . . even though I try to pretend I'm ok . . ." and "I just want to be happier because I know that's what my friends and family would want." We believe that as a result of taking the actions of recovery, you won't have to pretend you're okay, and you won't have to be happy to please others but will be able to do it for yourself.

From our hearts to yours,
Russell and John

I Have Morphed into Another Person; How Can I Recover?

Betsy from MS writes:
You talk of grief "recovery" but there's NO recovery from the death of a child. My son died two years ago and I will never "recover" because who I was before his death has disappeared and gone, vanished, and this other woman is left behind. If I have morphed into another person, how can I recover? I am this person now forever, a bereaved mother lost in a world of intact families. Perhaps I can learn to live despite the fact that my son is dead? No, never.

Dear Betsy,

I must start by saying that I have a special place in my heart for those of us who have experienced the death of a child. My son died in 1977 and at the time I thought and felt as you do now. I pray that you do not close your mind to the possibility of feeling better while at the same time never forgetting your son.

My issue back then was lack of knowledge about what actions to take in order to heal my heart. Now we know what very specific actions you can take to clear away the pain so that you are left with your fond memories.

Russell is going to give you some direction on where and how to start. Please do not give up on the idea of having a life of meaning and value even though the circumstances of your life have been changed forever.

If I were there with you, I would give you a hug.

John W. James

Dear Betsy,
Honestly, there's not a whole lot I can add to John's heartfelt note to you.

The writing of *The Grief Recovery Handbook* was the result of all the trials and experimentation John did to try to find a way to accommodate the emotionally impossible reality of the death of his son. In learning what he could do to deal with the death of all the *hopes, dreams, and expectations* he had for his son, and their life together, he uncovered some actions that helped him feel more emotionally complete, in spite of his broken heart.

Over the past thirty-five years, there have been many modifications and improvements to *The Grief Recovery Handbook* but one thing has remained the same, and that is the very first sentence which says: *If you are reading this book there is a high probability that your heart is broken.*

Believing that sentence is also true for you, we suggest that rather than focusing on whether or not recovery is possible, please read the book and see if what it says makes sense to you. Within the first 58 pages, which is Part One, you will have a clear idea of whether or not the book, and its content, can help you.

I join John in saying that if I were near you, I'd offer a hug.

From our hearts to yours,
Russell and John

When Is It Too Soon to Start Dating?

Berenice from CT writes:
When is it too soon to start a relationship after the death of your spouse?

Dear Berenice,

There's no "correct" answer to your question, though we'd guess people have given you all kinds of estimates. There is even an absurd mathematical equation you're liable to hear that says that you need to wait a year for every year you were married.

Our premise—along with our personal experiences—is that time is not the key factor in when a person should start dating after the death of a spouse. We know that time doesn't heal emotional wounds. We also know that many people have waited a year or two, or five or ten, or even twenty years after their spouses died, and the next relationship still failed. The majority of those failures were not necessarily because the two people didn't belong together, it was that the widow or widower was not emotionally complete with their spouse who had died. Absent that kind of completion, the new relationship is almost guaranteed to fail.

The other danger is that a person can "feel" ready to date or start a new relationship relatively soon after the death of their mate, but that feeling can be predicated on loneliness and other factors, not necessarily because they are emotionally complete with their spouse who died.

With that entire preamble, the time to start a new relationship is "after" having taken actions to discover and complete what was left emotionally unfinished in the earlier relationship. You'll notice that doesn't spell out any time zone at all, but that's not to say that a week after your spouse dies you should start dating. It's meant to indicate that it's the actions of completion that will dictate when you are ready to start a new relationship so you won't mix the old relationship in with the new one and sabotage it in advance.

After you take grief recovery actions you'll have a clearer sense of whether or not you're ready.

From our hearts to yours,
Russell and John

When Your Heart Is Broken Your Head Doesn't Work Right

Anonymous from NE writes:
I lost my son twelve years ago to Lymphoma and I have become very bitter and withdrawn. I can't find anything to occupy my time and nothing interests me. I can't seem to pull myself up out of this slump. He was our only child and I worshiped the ground he walked on—he was my world. When he died, I feel that our Pastor deserted us, so we had no spiritual counseling. I regret we didn't seek counseling elsewhere. Maybe if we did, I wouldn't be so bitter. Is it too late to seek counseling, or would it help since it's been so long?

Dear Anon,

There are several elements to your note, two of which compound what we believe to be the original issue—*your broken heart caused by the death of your son.* The two we want to address are the "spiritual counseling" and whether or not time heals emotional wounds.

When someone important to us dies, our hearts are broken—the heart being the symbolic word we all use to represent our emotions. While the spiritual component may be affected, it's not the key to our grief. The problem is that spiritual concepts do not repair our broken hearts. Without diminishing any good things that happened for you when you were being "spiritually counseled" by your pastor, whatever did take place didn't help you feel emotionally complete in relationship to your son who died. If it had, you wouldn't have written to us.

It's also accurate to say that when someone important to you dies, your intellectual aspect doesn't function well. We state it this way, "When your heart is broken your head doesn't work right; and when your heart is broken, your spirit (or other spiritual components) cannot soar."

The key to helping a broken heart is to learn the principles and take the actions that address the emotions that were left unfinished by the death.

Regarding time: Time can't heal a broken heart. In both cases, it requires correct actions. As you've observed, sadly, a full ten years hasn't healed your heart, and another ten, without recovery, will probably make it worse.

As a result of taking grief recovery actions, you will begin once more to want to involve yourself in life. It will also help you deal with your strong painful feelings about the pastor's actions—or nonactions. You will be able to retain the fond memories you have of your son. It will also allow you to remember him as you knew him in life, not only as you knew him in death; and it will allow you to redevelop a life of meaning and value even though it's dramatically different than what it might have been had he not died.

From our hearts to yours,
Russell and John

MYTH: BE STRONG FOR OTHERS: Q&A

The Real Key Is for *You* to Go First

Karen from WV writes:

My mom died about a month ago. She was my best friend and I miss her horribly. I seem to be dealing with it. I cry in the middle of the night sometimes, but I'm able to go on with my daily life. I am worried about my dad however. They were married fifty years and he's lost without her. He seems to go on with the daily mechanics of life, eating, bathing etc., but he's just a shell of himself and is starting to pull away from my children and me. If he comes over he doesn't stay long and if we go over there it's like he wants to rush us out. I've asked him about going to grief therapy but he refuses. He says he has to do it by himself. I'm afraid he'll just retreat into himself and not want anyone around. What can I do to help him? He's just so sad and broken.

Dear Karen,

Thank you for the truthful and concerned note. There are so many elements in your story. First and foremost is the missing of your mom, who was obviously so important in your life. We imagine she was the person you'd normally go to when your heart hurt, and now her absence is the cause of your pain.

We appreciate your concern for your dad and his wellbeing, but we'd guess the impact of his pulling away from you and your children is painful and frustrating for you and for them. We don't know the ages of your children, but we imagine they are confused and hurt by his apparent unavailability.

The problem is that he's probably pretty fixed in his ways, and one of his ways is to do it on his own. Unfortunately, every attempt you make to either help him or suggest he get help may push him further away.

The best thing you can do to help him, as strange as it may seem, is for you to help yourself with grief recovery actions. As you take them, something will start to shift in you, the way you talk about your feelings will change, and your dad will see that.

This *may* encourage him to open up and talk about what he's feeling.

The real key is for you to go first, not to try to get him to go first. The same is true with your kids—regardless of their ages.

From our hearts to yours,
Russell and John

A Tangled Web of Losses!

Shelley from ID writes:
My mother is eighty-five & suffering from dementia and serious health problems. Five years ago my dad died suddenly in her arms, and last year my brother was killed (the investigation is still ongoing). My brother hadn't had any contact with my mom for 20 years. Now my mom sits and cries and says, "He was my son." We try to comfort her, but with dementia we feel hopeless not knowing if our words reach her or not. She demands to know how he died and to date we don't know. How can we help her cope?

Dear Shelley,

Ouch, what a tangled web of losses—for you as well as for your mother. With dementia and Alzheimer's we lose that sense of connection with important people in our lives and the fact that they look and sound like who they "were" is very confusing. Even harder is trying to get them to be how they used to be, which of course doesn't happen.

You have at least three major losses over the past several years: the death of your father, the ongoing descent of your mother, and now the death of your brother. It's a good idea for you to start taking grief recovery actions to help you become as emotionally complete as you can in all three relationships. Working on mom while she is still alive will help you feel more complete with her as the person she was before the dementia set in and allow you to develop a new relationship with the woman she has become.

When it comes to your ongoing relationship with your mother: Rather than trying to comfort her which—as you can see—doesn't really work, tell the truth about yourself. Your truth about your brother and the mystery of his death might sound like this: "Yes, Mom, I'm also having a very hard time not knowing what happened. It sometimes keeps me awake at night as my imagination goes wild trying to guess. It also makes me sad when I realize that you and he didn't have any contact for so long."

It's not that we want her to comfort you instead of the other way around, what we want is for you and your mother to be able to be truthful in sharing whatever emotions are triggered by the death of your brother to the greatest degree possible.

The other guidance we suggest is that when your mother says, "He was my son," you might try saying, "Yes, Mom, I can't imagine how devastating it must be for you to not know what happened to him."

We believe that talking that way will be a much better thing than trying to comfort her. Even if she weren't afflicted with the dementia, comfort would not really work, as there's nothing you can say to ease someone else's emotional pain.

From our hearts to yours,
Russell and John

It's Amazing How Disconnected We Can Feel

Ginger from NJ writes:
My mother died about twenty years ago and my oldest sibling took over the responsibility of being mom to me and six other sisters and brothers. Three years ago one of my siblings died. I held on tightly to an older sister for support and then she died last year. I have one other sister but we are not as close as I was to this sister. I really don't want to live anymore, but again I have my own children and my two deceased sisters' children, totaling eight kids. I am so distraught and close to giving up but all these kids need me. How do I be strong?

Dear Ginger,

Thanks for being so totally honest about how overwhelmed you are with the responsibilities you've taken on and the burden of essentially doing it alone.

It's amazing how disconnected we can feel when some of the most important people in our lives die. It's not a surprise to us that you feel the way you do and, without them here for support, that life doesn't feel joyful for you.

We know a lot of people will tell you that you shouldn't feel that way. But we'd never say that because we have interacted with too many grieving people over the years who say many of the things you're saying.

While we can't bring back your sisters or your mom, we may be able to guide you to being able to get yourself back into your own life in a more positive way. We know that might seem impossible to you based on the way you feel right now, but we believe that if you give our suggestions a try, you might be surprised at the results.

We want to start by changing the language in your question, "How do I be strong?" When people say they need to "be strong" or "be strong for the children," we give them a new choice. We say, "You can be strong or you can be human. Pick one!"

When people try to "be strong" for others, they tend to hide their own feelings. When you do that in front of the children, they get confused because your body language doesn't match up to what they sense.

The best thing to do instead of trying to "be strong" is to "be emotionally honest." Tell the truth about yourself, especially when you're feeling sad. That not only will help you, but it will help teach the children how to be honest. If you just show them "strong" when it isn't truthfully how you feel, you'll be teaching them how to lie. We know that's not what you want to do.

One last thing: Since you have so many children under your wing, all of whom have been affected by grief, make sure you get a copy of our book, *When Children Grieve*. It will be of tremendous value for you as you guide the children through life and the inevitable losses that will happen.

From our hearts to yours,
Russell and John

Saying "I Know How You Feel" Robs Dignity from a Griever

Anonymous from MI writes:
What's the best way for me to support my daughter-in-law as she grieves over the sudden loss of her father?

Dear Anon,

Yours is an interesting question. Most people, in a loving attempt to be of service to grieving friends or family, say and do things that have the opposite effect. In part, they offer unsolicited advice, which causes the griever to want to run away and hide.

The biggest issue is that well-meaning, well-intended folks keep telling the griever *not to feel bad*. The problem is that feeling bad or feeling sad is the normal, and even healthy, reaction to the death of someone important to us.

You must resist the urge to say things like "Don't feel bad, he's in a better place." Or in the situation with the sudden death, "Don't feel bad, at least he didn't suffer a long illness." Also, please avoid saying "I know how you feel." Nothing robs dignity from a griever more than that comment.

Another thing you might find helpful is to encourage your daughter-in-law to tell you stories about her dad and about her relationship with him. That may help her a lot as she might be stuck on memories about the end of his life because of the sudden death. Having her talk about her lifetime with him will help her get unstuck from the ending.

Our best guidance to you is to simply be a "heart with ears." Don't analyze, criticize, or judge her, and definitely don't offer unsolicited opinions or advice.

From our hearts to yours,
Russell and John

Grieving People Need to Talk about What Happened

Melissa from NV writes:
The ex-wife of a close friend of mine died last week. He told me just before she died that he still loved her and was having regrets over their failed relationship. He just returned from the out-of-state funeral and I expect he'll be calling me in the near future. We're just good friends who enjoy our weekly teas and our discussions about history. My question is this: When he does call, what should I say? Should I mention the situation or just ignore it? I'm at a loss for words. I definitely am resolved not to call him because I don't know his state of mind at this time. Before he left, he was very upset.

Dear Melissa,

Obviously, it's not unusual for people to have regrets about a failed marriage, but we're not clear from your note if, when he told you before she died that he had those regrets, he already knew that she was terminally ill. That detail does to some degree affect what you might say to him when he returns.

Without knowing the answer, we'll give you some guidance based on other factors. Here's a basic truth: Grieving people need and want an opportunity to talk about "what happened" and about their relationship with the person involved.

With that in mind, you'd never want to rob your friend of that opportunity. Now that doesn't mean he would want to talk to you or me 24/7, but if you don't open the topic you might be doing him and your friendship a major disservice. If he doesn't want to talk, he won't—and you would just let that be okay with you.

As to you not calling him, we disagree. Since you know that his ex died, we'd recommend that you do. You could say something like: "I heard that your ex-wife died, and knowing that you'd told me you had some regrets about the end of that marriage, I wanted you to know I was thinking about you. I can't imagine what these past few weeks have been like for you." When you say that last part, make your voice go up at the end so it sounds like a gentle question, which is exactly what it is. It's an invitation to talk and he'll either accept it or not—his choice. He may not want to talk at that moment, but he will remember the offer.

The worst thing you can do is *not* bring up the topic of his ex-wife's death. We'd have to guess that he knows that you heard about it, and if so, and you don't mention it, he'll think you're avoiding the topic. Remember what we said above about grievers needing and wanting to talk about what happened. It's really the only thing on their minds and in their hearts.

As for being at a loss for words—that's absolutely true. It is impossible to know what to say because there are no universally correct things to say. Because that's true, one of the best things you could say is: "I heard your ex-wife died, and I don't know what to say." Since that is true for you, he will appreciate it and, by the time you talk to him, people will have said hundreds of incorrect and untruthful things to him—all with the intention of being helpful—and your comment will be a breath of fresh air.

From our hearts to yours,
Russell and John

Intervention Doesn't Work with The Grief Recovery Method®

Ed from OR writes:
My mother died three years ago and my father died last year. My younger sister has basically hijacked just about everything of sentimental value, along with everything else which, to the other five us, has no meaning at all. An old TV, my parents' pillows, their clothes, etc., you get the picture.

We're all in agreement that their home needs to be sold, but my sister has found a way to put a roadblock up at every turn. She just doesn't want to let go at all and every conversation turns to how much they are missed. We try to understand, but some of the behavior has begun to manifest itself in hoarding of possessions and animals. Every stray that passes by, she latches on to as if she's the only one who can care for the animal. We have suggested counseling but are rebuked angrily and have been told that we aren't the ones who are dealing with grief properly. It's gotten to the point where we don't feel comfortable around her anymore because of all of the references to my parents' favorite colors, their favorite foods, the list goes on. Everything reminds her of them and it's voiced over and over. If a person doesn't recognize they need help, how do you help them?

Dear Ed,
Thanks for your note, although we must say, we are very frustrated when we hear these kinds of stories—and we hear them all too often—because there's precious little we can do to help.

The problem is stated in no uncertain terms when you ask: "If a person doesn't recognize they need help, how do you help them?"

When it comes to grief recovery, we know that intervention doesn't work. If a participant is not willing, then the principles and actions of grief recovery—or anything else for that matter—will not work.

That said, the only thing we can suggest is that you do your own grief recovery work in relationship to each of your parents who have died, *and* in relationship to your living sister who is causing you no end of grief of a different kind.

While it's unlikely that you can get your sister to change her actions, you can modify *your* reactions and not continue to "give away your power" in response to what she does or says. As Eleanor Roosevelt famously said, "No one can make you feel inferior without your consent."

Ed, please understand that we hear you loud and clear and that we recognize that the situation you're dealing with is really horrible. We're also aware that the loss of the memorabilia that connects you to your familial past can be painful and acts as a constant reminder of the deaths.

All the more reason for you to do the work you need to do. Taking care of yourself is the best, and maybe the only, antidote to the situation you're in.

From our hearts to yours,
Russell and John

I'm Getting Tired of Propping Everyone Else Up

Anonymous from MA writes:
How do I respond to family members who seem critical of my grieving,
who tell me to "move on," "you're self-absorbed," "self-destructive,"
and other hurtful things?

This started the day of my wife's memorial service when I was told
I was "being rude" and "enabling myself to feel sad" because I cried
after reading the sympathy cards. They act as if I want to feel this way,
are disgusted, and want me to feel guilty. Do they really expect me to act
happy for their sake? I try, but I'm getting tired of propping everyone
else up. They have said/done nothing to comfort me in any way and
act as though my spouse never existed. It hurts a great deal and isn't
helping me heal any.

Dear Anon,
Sadly, your note and questions represent something very common for many grievers. It's heartbreaking that the person with
the broken heart has to try to take care of the very people who
should be more conscious, aware, and helpful to them. The most
important thing in the situation is to find at least a few people
you can trust so that when you want and need to talk about what
you're experiencing, you won't feel judged or criticized.

When the "less than helpful or courteous" ones say things
that you find hurtful, the best advice is to not bite back at them.
You don't want to waste your energy being distracted from the
real feelings of grief that signify your emotional relationship
with your wife who died.

What we've done in similar personal circumstances is just to
say to anyone whose comments didn't sit well with us, "Thank
you, we really appreciate your concern," and then get away from
that person. We, too, need to remember that even though by
profession we are grief recovery educators, when someone important to us dies, we are grievers, not teachers.

The best and only real gift we can give you is to say, "We hear you, loud and clear." And, if you want to send us email from time to time, we will do our utmost to acknowledge it and, more importantly, the feelings you express.

From our hearts to yours,
Russell and John

MYTH: BE STRONG FOR OTHERS

All Relationships Are Unique

Rita from AR writes:
I have a twin sister whose only daughter died four years ago. Her boy-friend shot her. It's been very tough on us all, and I still have a hard time coping, but my sister is stuck in anger mode and there's no moving her. She's so far into it that there's no talking to her at all. All reason has been pushed aside. She says no one understands because it was her daughter and we don't know what she's going through. She's very destructive towards the emotions of others. Now my mother has been diagnosed with cancer and her anger has intensified. Can you help? I cry every day still, but now it's not just for my niece, but for my sister too! Thank you so much for your time, and for listening.

Dear Rita,
Indeed, for you the loss is compounded if you've lost your sister on top of the death of your niece. And, knowing that twins can be exceptionally close—whether identical or fraternal—we'd imagine that your pain is overwhelming. Then there's your mother's diagnosis as well.

There's no easy answer we can give you. No matter what we say that might be helpful for you, we aren't able to talk to your sister and, as you probably already know, she wouldn't listen to us or be able to hear us at this point anyway. Her anger—as under-standable as it may be—keeps her away from any kind of help or comfort from family or friends, and certainly keeps her far away from the guidance of professionals.

The only thing you can do is take care of yourself. You need to take the actions that will help you feel as emotionally com-plete as you can with your niece AND with your sister. In addi-tion to that helping you, the best we can then hope for is that at some point she'll notice the change in you and will ask about it. Until then, since she's not asking for your help (or anyone else's), you have to leave her alone.

The fact is that no one does understand how she feels; even another woman whose daughter was killed in the exact same manner wouldn't understand because all relationships are unique.

As you take the actions in *The Grief Recovery Handbook*, you'll get back some of your energy, which we're guessing you might need if you're to be one of the primary caregivers for your mother.

From our hearts to yours,
Russell and John

The Word "Imagine" Creates Safety

Caitlin from ID writes:

My teenage daughter died twenty years ago. It was a long hard struggle but I'm okay now. My grief was so strong that I don't even remember how I moved on. My friends'17-year-old recently died in a tragic car accident. I want to reach out to them but I'm not certain of the best way to do this. I know what I feel and believe today is a whole spectrum away from what I felt then and I don't know how to help them because I wasn't feeling at all then. I know they are in deep despair and grief and I want to help them. I especially don't want their marriage to disintegrate. Both are such nice people. Please guide me so that I may help them.

Dear Caitlin,

We're touched about your concern for your friends, and indeed for their marriage, which could be negatively affected by this tragedy. One of the issues with grief recovery is that "intervention" is not advisable. That is, we can't force people to do what we know would help them. It requires willing participation.

That said, we also don't know if either the husband or the wife has reached out and asked you for help. And we don't know if either of them is aware that you had a daughter die a long time ago. What you can do is tell the truth about yourself, which is that you can say, "Even though I had a daughter die many years ago, I can't imagine what this has been like for you." As you say that, you make your voice go up at the end, to turn what is really a statement into a gentle question. It's the safest and most helpful way to ask, "How are you feeling?" without actually saying that phrase.

That gentle invitation to talk is almost always met with an open and honest response. In part, because the word "imagine" suggests that you will listen to whatever they say without judgment, analysis, or opinion, thereby making it safe to talk to you.

Hopefully they will trust you and talk a little about what they're experiencing. Keep that conversation short and when you feel the moment is right, you can introduce them to *The Grief Recovery Handbook*. We suggest you read at least the first 58 pages (Part One) before doing so. Then, you can offer them your copy of the book with the following statement: "Here's a book that I found to be really helpful. I thought you might benefit from it also." By doing it that way, you're not suggesting that there's anything wrong with them, just that they might find something of value in the book.

Hopefully, as they read those pages, they'll get a sense of hope that recovery is possible, and they'll move towards taking the actions the book outlines.

One caution: The book calls for people to work in pairs. However, it's never a good idea for husband and wife to work together, especially since they had different and unique relationships with their son who died. This is a circumstance where you might volunteer to be partner with one of them in the process the book outlines.

You are free to contact us as this unfolds for any guidance we can provide.

From our hearts to yours,
Russell and John

CHAPTER
FIVE

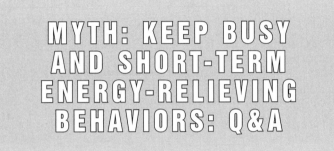

MYTH: KEEP BUSY AND SHORT-TERM ENERGY-RELIEVING BEHAVIORS: Q&A

STERBs—What Are They?

Many people are surprised to find themselves with a great deal of emotional energy even a substantial time after the death of someone important to them. While grief clearly can seem to drain energy and exhaust you, it also seems to create energy, which you may or may not realize is a product or by-product of the emotions caused by the death of someone important to you.

The impact of the six myths about grief complicates matters. They suggest that we shouldn't feel the way we're feeling; that we shouldn't burden others with those feelings; and that we should be strong rather than being human. As a result of those beliefs, we don't have an effective way of expressing the abundance of emotional energy that builds up in us in the days, weeks, and months after the death of someone important in our lives. Whether we're aware of it or not, we start to participate in various behaviors or activities that we call Short-Term Energy-Relieving Behaviors or *STERBs*.

The most classic STERB is the use of food, closely followed by alcohol and drugs. There are many others, including: fantasy (movies, TV, books, Internet), exercise, sex, isolation, anger, shopping (otherwise known as retail therapy), work, gambling, and many more.

STERBs are the indirect things we do to try to deal with our feelings, but since we don't address them head-on, they don't work. For example, if you have a fight with your spouse and, because you're upset, you eat a quart of ice cream, you haven't done anything to deal with your hurt feelings and, worse, you now have to deal with the aftermath of your overeating.

Using STERBs creates the illusion that you're addressing the feelings caused by the death of someone important to you. Not only do they not work, but also, as we indicated in the ice cream example, there are all kinds of problems that can accrue as a result. An even larger problem is that neither food nor alcohol, nor any of the dozens of other activities you might engage in as STERBs, help you become emotionally complete with the person who died. So people eat more, drink more, or distract themselves on the computer or in front of the TV more, but they don't deal with their emotions caused by the death. Without any direct action to deal with the emotions caused by the death, they just keep getting worse.

Many STERBs are a by-product of the myth, "Keep Busy." Since we don't always know how to deal effectively with the emotions caused by the loss events in our lives, we sometimes fall back on the myths that we learned along the way. We may not realize we're doing it, but many activities that would fall under the heading of "Keeping Busy" could also be called STERBs.

Many of the questions and answers in this section revolve around the misuse of STERBs. As you'll see when you read them, we are always trying to help people realize the danger and futility of using STERBs and give them courage to take actions of recovery.

Grief Is Exhausting!

Mallory from SC writes:
My sister's husband died in July. I have been staying with her every
weekend since it happened. She's alone in her house with their dogs. She
never stops cleaning or taking care of the animals. She never relaxes. She
stays busy, doesn't sleep very well. How can I get her to take time out for
herself? She's so lost without him. He did EVERYTHING for her. And I
do mean everything. He cooked, cleaned, took care of the bills . . . I mean
everything. What can I do? I have gone over early and cleaned for her so
she would not have to but she will not relax. Does she need more time? I
know it's only been 4 months, but I am very worried about her and her
mental state. I talk to her every day. What can I say to help?

Dear Mallory,
Grief and unresolved grief create enormous amounts of emotional energy—while at the same time draining energy and exhausting the griever. In *The Grief Recovery Handbook* we use an ac-
ronym, *STERBs*, as shorthand for Short-Term Energy-Relieving
Behaviors. What you describe, in terms of your sister's incredible
output of energy (cleaning, taking care of the dogs, etc.) is a
perfect example of a STERB, which is a very normal and natural
reaction to a major grief-producing event.

We have little doubt that her husband's death has been the
most life-shattering event in her life and that his absence creates
volumes of energy that she's trying to dispel—not knowing what
else to do with it all. Time won't heal her broken heart any more
than time would put air back into a flat tire. As with a flat tire, actions are required to get the car back on the road and actions are
required to get her heart back into the mainstream of life—even
without him here.

Rather than there being something you can say to help,
there's something you can do. If you get a copy of *The Grief*
Recovery Handbook and read at least the first 58 pages (Part One),

then you can give the book to your sister with this statement: "I have found this book to be very helpful, I thought you would benefit from it also." Saying it that way will prevent her from thinking that you're saying there's something wrong with her.

We want to mention that you're very correct when you say it's *only* been four months, and her grief is probably still very raw. While we did indicate that time can't heal a broken heart, adapting to the painful, new, unwanted reality of the death of someone important to us happens within time and is usually accompanied by a host of STERBs, and a very diminished emotional and physical state.

From our hearts to yours,
Russell and John

How Do I Deal with the Anger I Feel?

Anonymous from WA writes:

My husband died unexpectedly three years ago and I'm still grieving very deeply. There are days when I just can't function at all and others where I just get by. It seems that I'll never get over the anger at both him and God. I talk with friends and see a counselor but neither seems to make much difference. Is this normal? What can I do to help the deep depression and sadness that I feel? It seems the only way I can cope is to sleep or get lost in watching TV.

Dear Anon,

Thanks for your note and question. There are a couple of major elements in your email that we want to address. STERBs, or Short-Term Energy-Relieving Behaviors, are the things we do as grievers that seem to relieve or dispel some of the overwhelming buildup of emotional energy that is caused by the death of the person for whom we are grieving. The problem with STERBs is built into the first part: short-term. There's no long-term relief when we just use up energy to distract us from our pain—it doesn't make it go away.

Among the most common short-term relievers is anger. The problem with anger is that you can never finish or complete it. It just keeps looping, like a hamster on a wheel. The more time you spend using your energy to express the anger, the less time you spend on what would help you discover and resolve what was left emotionally unfinished for you by your husband's untimely death.

The other issues you brought up are also among the most typical STERBs—sleeping and spending endless hours watching TV (or, in some cases, reading escapist novels). Those nonaction activities also do nothing to help you discover and complete what was left emotionally unfinished for you because of your husband's sudden death.

If you take grief recovery actions, you'll finally have the opportunity to complete the pain and anger you feel. We cannot help you get your husband back, but we can help you get your heart back and have a life of meaning and value even though he's gone.

From our hearts to yours,
Russell and John

Memorial Jewelry Doesn't Heal Your Heart

Kelsey from FL writes:
My brother died a year ago. We were very close and I seem not to get
better. I've been in and out of deep depressions. He had a lot of illnesses
before he died. I blame myself a lot. I have tons of dreams about him,
where just before I tell him how I feel about him, I wake up. I have
started hurting myself. It's the only way I can deal with the pain I feel
inside. I cry more than I should. I have also started drinking every time
I think about him. I have a necklace with his ashes in it. I thought it
would make me feel better, but it just made me feel worse than I did
before I got it.

Dear Kelsey,
Many people are surprised to find themselves with a great deal
of emotional energy even a substantial time after the death of
someone important to them. While a year is not a very long
time to still be experiencing emotions about the death of your
brother, we're more concerned with some of the things you're
doing in an attempt to deal with those feelings.

In our books, we talk about various behaviors or activities
grieving people participate in which we call STERBs or Short-
Term Energy-Relieving Behaviors. The most classic STERBs are
food, closely followed by alcohol and drugs. One of the less common ones is hurting oneself. We don't perceive it to be pathologi-
cal, any more than using food or alcohol, though there can be
some scary consequences. You talked about hurting yourself and
about using alcohol to deal with the feelings, and we're pretty
sure from the tone and content of your note that neither of those
has given you any long-term relief from your grief. That's why
we call them *short-term* energy relievers.

On a different topic, in your note you say: "He had a lot of
illnesses before he died. I blame myself a lot." We were a little
confused as to whether you think you somehow did something

to cause those illnesses. If not, then what you say is not accurate and you may be giving yourself a lot of feeling about something you didn't cause. That's not to say that you can't feel sad about the medical conditions he suffered with, but if you didn't cause them, don't give yourself any more painful feelings than you already have—which are plenty.

Regarding your comment, "I cry more than I should." Since every grieving person is unique and different, we don't know what the right amount of crying is, so we don't know why you would be upset with yourself for having a lot of *normal* and *natural* emotions related to the death of your brother—especially when you say that you "were very close."

Finally, as to the necklace with his ashes inside: That kind of memorial jewelry can have a wonderfully emotional value but, as you've discovered, it doesn't heal your heart any more than hurting yourself or drinking do.

With those items addressed, at least a little, we strongly recommend that you go to the library or bookstore and get a copy of *The Grief Recovery Handbook*. As you read it and start taking the actions it outlines you should start feeling a shift and, hopefully, you'll move away from those STERBs which aren't doing you any good. You'll find the section on STERBs at pages 77–82 of the *Handbook*.

From our hearts to yours,
Russell and John

Keeping Busy Just Exhausts Us

Dolores from MN writes:

I am a Christian but have lost a lot it seems, and I'm just not sure what to do anymore. After fourteen years of marriage, my husband committed suicide after our divorce. That was ten years ago, and I never remarried. My mother died three years ago and now my father and my best friend a few weeks ago. I have two wonderful daughters, am only 48 years old, and feel very lost. I work hard and try staying busy, but at the end of the day I mostly cry myself to sleep. I feel tired of hurting but am not sure how, besides praying every few minutes, to find happiness.

Dear Dolores,

Thanks for your note. It must seem overwhelming to you to have had so many people die within a relatively short time. Not to mention the feelings you probably had—and still have—about your ex-husband and that he ended his own life.

There are six myths we write and talk about that affect many grievers. One of those myths is the idea that it's helpful to "Keep Busy" in an attempt to deal with the tremendous amount of emotion generated by the deaths of people who are important to us.

The problem with "keeping busy" is that it does nothing at all to complete the unfinished emotions caused by the death, and the unrealized *hopes, dreams, and expectations* we had for our future with that person. And, worse, "keeping busy" just exhausts us. When it doesn't fix our broken hearts, we begin to think that something's wrong with us.

Prayer is wonderful but, like "keeping busy," it doesn't complete unfinished business nor does it fix our broken hearts. Like a group of behaviors we call STERBs, or Short-Term Energy-Relieving Behaviors, prayer can offer temporarily relief, but some additional actions are necessary. We hope you'll find the energy to do some grief recovery work so you can create a shift in how you feel.

From our hearts to yours,
Russell and John

You Can't Bypass Feelings, You Have to Go through Them

Francis from GA writes:
My husband died eight weeks ago after a three-month illness at the age of 59. I don't know what to do to get away from myself. Should I help others in similar circumstances? My constant self-absorption and feelings of sadness have become tiresome and depressing. I'm an artist and financially independent. Any ideas at this point would be appreciated.

Dear Francis,

At only eight weeks after the death of your spouse, we would not consider your feelings of sadness to be self-absorption. In fact, we would say that for the most part, it is well within the range of normal and natural to be having that experience. We would also say that the raw grief of adapting to a new, painful, unwanted reality is a difficult and exhausting experience. Rather than fighting the feelings and labeling them as you have, we suggest you confront them straight up. As cliché as this might sound, you can't go over, under, or around your feelings—you have to go through them.

The primary response to the death of someone important to us, especially our spouse, is fear. That fear manifests itself in an obvious question, "What will happen to me?" While it may seem self-centered, it is really an honest survival question. As you understand that, we hope you will be a little gentler about your own normal reactions to your husband's death.

We don't recommend that grieving people try to help other grievers as a way of distracting themselves from their own feelings. We do suggest that you get a copy of *The Grief Recovery Handbook*—available in most libraries and bookstores. As you read it you'll discover a thing we call STERBs, which stands for Short-Term Energy-Relieving Behaviors.

STERBs are the things people do in an attempt to deal with the overwhelming emotions connected to grief. But STERBs do not address the unfinished emotional business that's attached to our relationships with people who have died.

The Grief Recovery Handbook will guide you in the actions that will help you feel more complete and, in turn, the sadness and excess energy will diminish.

From our hearts to yours,
Russell and John

The Ongoing Controversy: The Alleged Stages of Grief vs. Typical, Normal, and Natural Responses to Loss

Most people are familiar with the phrase "Stages of Grief," though they may not realize that the original concept and phrase was "Stages of Dying." Coined in the mid-1960s by Dr. Elisabeth Kübler-Ross in her famous book *On Death and Dying,* the good doctor's life work and writing humanized how dying people were treated, and became a foundation component of the then-fledgling hospice movement. For all that she did, she is to be honored and appreciated.

Sadly, in our opinion, an accidental by-product of her work was the morphing and misunderstanding of "Stages of Dying" into "Stages of Grief," a transition we believe has harmed many more people than it has helped. In part, that's because the stages theory related to grief is not "normal and natural" and puts grieving people in conflict with what is true for them.

Chapter Six explains in some detail why we believe there are no stages of grief, and how the belief that such stages do exist can distance grieving people from their normal, natural, and healthy responses to the death of someone important to them. Following this are actual letters that relate to the misapplication of the stages of grief to natural responses—which don't occur in a given time frame.

The balance of Part Two is devoted to questions that are based on naturally occurring issues that affect grievers: Crying or Not Crying, Being Robbed of Saying Goodbye, and a variety of other concerns.

ARE THERE ACTUAL STAGES OF GRIEF?

We are often asked if there are actual stages of grief or grieving. The answer is NO! There are no stages of grief or grieving. Even though you may hear or read that there are such stages, there is no predictable progression of feelings and thoughts that applies to any one person, much less to a group of people.

Every relationship is unique. Therefore the feelings you have when someone important to you dies are also unique. Any attempt to quantify your emotional reaction to the death of someone important to you may keep you from taking the actions that will help you deal with your unique reaction to the death of that person.

Why do people think there are stages? Many years ago Elisabeth Kübler-Ross wrote a book entitled *On Death and Dying*. The book identified five stages that a *dying person* might go through after being told they had a terminal illness. Those stages are: denial, anger, bargaining, depression, and acceptance. For many years, in the absence of more accurate information, well-meaning people incorrectly assigned the stages about dying people to the *grief* people feel when someone important to them dies.

It's fair to say that following a death, grievers may feel sad, and they might have some anger about the circumstances or cause of the death, or even about things that did or didn't happen in their relationship with the person who died. But those are feelings, they are not stages.

They are normal and natural emotional reactions to a death. They don't happen in any predetermined order, if they occur at all. If we start with an incorrect premise, we will wind up far away from the truth. *The idea that stages of grief even exist is dangerous.*

After all, a griever is often in a very suggestible condition—dazed, numb, walking in emotional quicksand. Many grievers are told that they are *in denial.* Yet in all our years working with tens of thousands of grievers, we've never met anyone *in denial* that a loss had occurred. They say, "Since my mom died, I've had a hard time." There's no denial in that comment. There's a very clear acknowledgment that there's been a death, and that there's been an emotional impact.

What about anger? Often when a death has occurred there's no anger at all, as this story explains: "I had a wonderful relationship with my grandmother. At age 92, she got ill and died. Blessedly, it happened quickly, so she did not suffer very much. I'm pleased about that. I had just spent some time with her sharing memories and saying how much we cared about each other. I'm very happy about that. The funeral ceremony created a truly accurate memory picture of her, and people came and talked about her. I loved that. A friend reminded me to say any last things to her and then say goodbye, and I did, and I'm glad. I think of her often with fondness and sometimes with a tear in my eye and I cherish those feelings. I am aware of the wonderful memories of my relationship with the incredible woman who was my grandma, and I miss her. And, I am not angry."

Unresolved Grief Is about Undelivered Emotional Communications

Unresolved grief is about undelivered communications of an emotional nature. It's about the things we wish we had said or done *differently, better, or more*; and it's about the unrealized *hopes, dreams, and expectations* for the future. It can also be about the things we wish the other person had said or done, or even had not said or done.

The fact is that there are many feelings that may be attached to those unsaid things. Happiness, sadness, love, fear, anger, relief, and compassion are just some of the feelings that a griever might experience. We don't need to categorize, analyze, or explain those feelings. We do need to learn how to communicate them and then say goodbye to the physical relationship that has been ended by the death.

It's most important to understand that there are no absolutes. There are no definitive stages or time zones for grieving. Grief is the normal and natural reaction to loss. Grief is emotional, not intellectual. Rather than defining stages of grief, which could easily confuse a griever, we prefer to help each griever find their own truthful expression of the thoughts and feelings that may be keeping them from participating in their own lives. We all bring different and varying beliefs to the losses that occur in our lives, therefore we each perceive and feel differently about each loss.

Please don't let anyone label your feelings as stages.

Note: In a most interesting statement in the introduction to her book, *Question & Answers on Death and Dying*, Kübler-Ross states: "I have specifically excluded chapters on 'Religion and Life after Death' as well as chapters on 'Bereavement and Grief.' This was done not only because of lack of space, but because there are others who are more qualified to answer those questions."

For an even more in-depth look at the idea of there being no stages of grief, please visit our website www.griefrecovery method.com and read the article "The Myth of the Stages of Dying, Death, and Grief."

NO STAGES OF GRIEF: Q&A

Statement of Death Is NOT Denial

Anonymous from CT writes:
My cousin killed himself over a year ago, and I am still in a state of denial. Is that normal after a year?

Dear Anon,
Language can be an important influence on how we feel. When you say your cousin killed himself over a year ago, you're making a clear statement that he is dead. There's absolutely no denial in that. It's better to speak in terms of emotional truths that can help you adapt to this loss. For example, "I'm having a really hard time since my cousin died. I can't focus, and I'm haunted by the images of him at the end of his life."

As you can see, we made up some thoughts and feelings about what you may be feeling. We'd guess that some of them are accurate for you. We did that to give you better language that will allow you to move off the idea of denial and towards the idea of recovery.

The actions of grief recovery will help you discover and complete what was left emotionally unfinished for you with his death.

From our hearts to yours,
Russell and John

Adapting to the Painful Reality of Death

Margot from CA writes:
Will I ever realize that he's gone?

Dear Margot,
Sad, sweet question. The fact is that you already realize that he's gone. It's built into the last words of your question. Of course it's very, very difficult to adapt to the painful, unwanted reality of the death of someone important to you. Please notice that we said "adapt to" as opposed to "accept."

One suggestion is to make small and accurate comments to others or to yourself as feelings come up for you. Example, "At this moment, I feel very sad and alone, and I miss him very much." By saying "At this moment," which would be honest, you don't make the feeling last longer than it needs to. Some people say "I feel depressed today" and extend the pain or sadness way beyond the moment they felt it.

From our hearts to yours,
Russell and John

Has the Reality of My Loss Set in Yet?

Indira from WA writes:

My mother died a week ago and I've returned home from taking care of her apartment, car, possessions, and her life. My mom was only 45 years old and I am 22. I'm worried that the reality of my loss has not quite set in yet. My sleep patterns and appetite have been affected tremendously. I feel physical pain plus odd muscle twinges I didn't have before. I'm not abusing alcohol or drugs. I was always the strong one in the family and the one who took care of everything and everyone.

My question is: If I feel numb, am I still grieving? I was only angry for a few days following her death and now I am just sad—more than sad. I understand that this is a traumatic experience but I am worried that the pain I feel will hit me all at once and render me incapable of living the life of a fully functioning adult. Do you think that is a reasonable worry? Thank you for the help.

Dear Indira,

Thank you for your email and questions. We want to focus on one particular part of your note, where you say: "I'm worried that the reality of my loss has not quite set in yet." You're probably very correct in that assumption. Years ago we coined a phrase, "emotional Novocain," to explain the fact that our body / mind package will shut down to protect us from feeling the amount and intensity of pain caused by the death of someone important to us, particularly with a sudden or unexpected death. Although you didn't mention the cause of your mother's death, or whether it was sudden or the result of a long illness, the sense of unreality also applies when a death is out of scope in time, as must be the case when a woman of forty-five dies.

Grieving people often seem to be able to get through the first week or ten days after a death, but are surprised at what happens to them after that, when the full reality of the loss hits them. It's also important to note that the initial reaction, in which the reality doesn't seem to have hit, is not the famous "'denial'" that is alluded to in the alleged stages a dying person might go through. It's really a protective survival response that gives you the time and ability to adapt to the painful reality of the death.

Even though numbness is a normal and typical reaction, not knowing that's true sometimes causes grievers to think there's something wrong with them, or that they are crazy. Nothing could be further from the truth.

As you absorb what we've just said, it's important for you to understand that what's going on—including your legitimate sense that it hasn't hit you yet—is also normal and natural. That said, you would be well advised to make sure you have people you trust who you can talk to when the reality of your feelings comes crashing to the surface. The more you can speak about what you're experiencing, the more you will reduce the possibility of something emotionally or physically negative happening to you, and the less liable you are to be rendered incapable of functioning.

To read more on this topic please see our article, "Normal and Natural Reactions to Death," on page 247.

From our hearts to yours,
Russell and John

Your Broken Heart Talking!

Janice from KY writes:
Last year my husband of less than two years died. We were high school sweethearts. My first question is when will I stop feeling that he is away and is going to be right back? Even though I've been through the funeral process, I still have this feeling. Will it ever leave?

Also, my kids are really starting to ask if I'm going to move on to another relationship. I don't understand the length of the grieving cycle and the different stages. I don't want to meet someone new until I'm sure I'm emotionally and mentally complete, and ready. What is a normal time frame for a widow to grieve?

Dear Janice,

Thanks for your note and your two questions. Both of them relate to time zones that no one can definitively answer. Compounding the problem is that most people have been led to believe that time heals all wounds, but it doesn't because it can't—time can only pass. And when time doesn't heal, it seems to get worse. When we read your first question, we immediately realized that you're trapped in the idea that at some point in time those feelings and thoughts about him just being off on an errand and coming right back will lift and your life will change. But the sad end of your question, "Does this feeling ever leave?" indicates that it's not getting better and is probably getting worse.

In fairness to you, we believe that those feelings represent your "broken heart talking," and that you miss him very much. To be sad and to miss someone you love is normal and even healthy.

Until or unless you take some actions to complete what was left emotionally unfinished by his death, it's unlikely that anything will change for you. The good news is that there are actions that can help you discover and complete what was left emotionally incomplete for you when your husband died.

We believe that as a partial result of taking grief recovery actions, the sense of him just being away for a while will diminish and allow you to restart the rest of your life. You may still love him and miss him but you will be able to move forward, and you will be able to be emotionally and mentally ready and available to be in a new relationship—if you choose to do that—and not sabotage it with the unfinished business from your past. As we indicated earlier, there are no "'normal'" time zones for grief—for widows or anyone else, and there are no pre-set stages.

From our hearts to yours,
Russell and John

He Won't See Me Graduate, Get Married, or Have Kids

Cathy from MN writes:
I'm only sixteen and I'm not sure how this works—if someone who actually cares is reading this or not. I know there are stages of grief. In truth, I don't know what "stage" I'm at (if there really are stages of grief anyway). I'm not an open person and most of my friends don't even know about my dad's death last year. I think I might need to talk to someone because it might help me turn my life back around for the good. I don't think I will ever feel normal again. I watched my father die and I was the second to last person to talk to him. He won't see me graduate, get married, or have kids. I feel trapped because I don't want to talk to my brothers or mother or friends about it.

Dear Cathy,
Someone who cares IS reading this. Based on your comment about someone actually caring, we can easily guess that people aren't listening to you anymore—assuming that they may have listened a little in the first weeks and months after your dad died. It's beyond sad when someone important to us dies, but it's compounded when people have to go outside of their own family or social circle just to be heard.

"He won't see me graduate, get married, or have kids." That's a powerful statement because so much of unresolved grief has to do with the unrealized *hopes, dreams, and expectations* for the future. Although those may be accurate truths about your future, you have to become emotionally complete with that reality so you can move forward and, as you say, "Help me turn my life back around for the good . . ."

"Emotionally complete" might sound like only words to you, but we assure you that if you take the actions of grief recovery, you'll begin to feel a shift which will allow you to begin to feel normal again, even though your life is and will be different without your dad here.

We don't agree with the idea that there are set stages of grief, and separating yourself into categories of time can actually impede the recovery process.

From our hearts to yours,
Russell and John

I Desperately Need to Know How to Live Again

Rita from NJ writes:
My three-year-old son died six months ago from a condition that he was
born with. Doctors told me it would happen, but he fought his way back
from multiple hospitalizations and complications. I just knew he would
be with me forever. I haven't accepted it, and I desperately need to know
how to live again.

Dear Rita,
We're sure you realize that in addition to the pure, raw grief of
missing your son, his death ended the *hopes, dreams, and expectations* for his future and your life with him. We believe that's a
huge part of what makes you feel that you haven't accepted his
death, and keeps you from moving forward with your life.

The only way we know to help restore people's willingness
and ability to begin to "live again" is to encourage them to take
the actions of grief recovery which help them discover and complete everything they wish had been *different, better, or more;* and
to address all the unrealized *hopes, dreams, and expectations* for
their future.

Of course doing the work cannot bring your son back, but it
can help you get your heart back and with it the will and drive to
get back into life. Please note that doing the work will not erase
any fond memories you have of your son and the relationship
you had with him.

From our hearts to yours,
Russell and John

ON CRYING: Q&A

I Still Cry Daily. Is that Normal?

Jimmy from MO writes:
My dad died four years ago. I took care of him and sort of put my life on hold. I'm 45 and single and all alone. I can't get over him not being here. I still cry daily. Is that normal?

Dear Jimmy,
Thanks for your note and of course we're sorry to hear of your father's death. You pose an interesting question that doesn't have a simple answer. If you'd said you smile daily remembering things you enjoyed about your dad and your relationship with him, you probably wouldn't be asking if that was normal. By the same token, missing someone and crying is not all that different. From that point of view it is normal to be sad when we miss someone who's no longer physically here. There's no limit on how often or how much we feel sad.

As to your comment about crying daily: We assume that when you cry about your dad, the sadness you feel is emotionally painful for you. If so, it's important that you discover and complete what may have been left emotionally unfinished in your relationship with him. As you do that, you'll most likely find that the kind of painful sadness you have felt will diminish and the frequency of those sad or painful feelings will also lessen.

The actions of The Grief Recovery Method® will help you discover and complete unfinished emotions, and the sooner you take those actions, the sooner you'll find changes in how you feel. The actions will not cause you to forget your dad, nor will they limit any fond memories. Pain is the feeling we're trying to help you deal with, while leaving the normal feelings of sadness and joy.

From our hearts to yours,
Russell and John

Force Myself to Cry to Make People Stop Worrying about Me?

Libby from NV writes:
I'm fifteen and my mom just died. I overheard my school counselors talk-
ing and they're worried about me because I haven't cried. I still miss her,
but when I cry, it hurts. It makes my eyes burn bad and makes me feel
like throwing up. When I was younger, if I got mad or one of my pets
died, my mom would tell me not to cry because I'd make myself sick.
I don't think I should cry now either. What can I do other than force
myself to cry to make people stop worrying about me?

Dear Libby,

This is very delicate for us to have to say, but your mom, in an apparent attempt to help you when you were little, created the idea that if you were sad and cried you'd make yourself sick, and now, that's exactly what's happening.

Over the years, we've helped many people who could not or would not cry for reasons similar to yours, and sometimes for other reasons. We don't try to get them to cry, because "not crying" can be a very strong belief system and it also becomes a habit. Even though you're very young, you have strong beliefs and habits about sad feelings and this affects how you deal with loss.

Rather than trying to get you to cry, we'd encourage you to tell the truth about how you feel. When you wrote, "I still miss her," that's all we needed to hear to know that you're emotionally affected by your mother's death. We assume you're sad, and we'd imagine you have many other feelings as well. Our concern isn't whether you ever cry, but whether you try to force feelings to stay inside of you. We've known many people who made themselves sick because they didn't tell the truth about how they felt—with or without crying.

We also have a funny feeling that it might be difficult for you to think about and talk about your mom and the feelings you're having without crying. Since crying is so fearful for you, you're trapped. You have a problem if you don't cry, and you have a problem if you do.

For now, we want you to know that there's nothing wrong with you. We believe you're a young woman whose heart is broken because her mother died. Please feel free to share this email with your counselors, and if they wish to contact us, we'd be glad to talk with them. We agree with you that it would be a bad idea to force yourself to cry to get them off your back. If you do cry, it should be because it's normal and natural for you when speaking about your mother.

If you want to read more about crying, you'll find two articles we wrote, "On Crying—Part One" and "On Crying—Part Two," on pages 242 and 244. Also, if you're able to get *The Grief Recovery Handbook* from the library, it will really help you deal with the dramatic changes in your life caused by your mother's death.

From our hearts to yours,
Russell and John

Death of a Spouse Can Be Like Losing a Piece of Your Body

Jason from MN writes:
My mother, father, and wife all died last year within 3 months of each other! I miss them so much, but the question I have is: Why am I able to deal with the loss of my mom and dad so much better than I can with the loss of my wife? I cry every day about her. Is this normal? I have been trying to find an answer, but I come up with nothing.

Dear Jason,

While we never compare losses, it's very common to hear people report, as you do, that the death of their spouse seemed to affect them emotionally more or for much longer time than the deaths of their parents. There is a kind of logic to that even though emotions can't be measured in logical or rational terms.

In long-term marital relationships you have chosen to be with your partner every day for many years, perhaps forty, fifty, sixty, or more. The effect of that amount of time with another person is almost like joining two people together and when one of them dies, it can literally feel like losing a piece of your body.

On the other hand, as we get older, we also have very long-term relationships with our living parents and those relationships are as many years as we've been alive. If you're sixty, you have a sixty-year relationship with your eighty-five-year-old mother. However, there's usually a major difference between your relationship with a parent and the one with your spouse: Most of us move away from home after high school or college and go off to build our careers and our marriages. So even though we may have a sixty-year relationship with a parent, we usually only lived with them for the first eighteen to twenty-two years of our lives. With our long-term spouses, we have spent nearly every day for fifty or sixty years with that person and the bond, even with a spouse we may have bickered with for much of the time, is incredibly strong. It may seem obvious, but it still has to be said that the nature of marriage is different than the relationships between parents and children.

You didn't mention how long you'd been married, but even when a marriage didn't last many decades, the nature and intensity of a marital relationship is differently intense than other relationships, and can produce overwhelming emotions of grief when one partner dies. None of that is said to diminish or minimize the amount of love and other feelings we have for our parents.

As to the second part of your question: Yes, it's normal to cry every day over the death of your wife. Obviously, that usually stops for most people after a few weeks or months. The problem is that there is no time zone that would apply to everyone as to how long daily crying should last. Since it has been more than a year, and since you mention it as something that concerns you, you may be stuck in your grief. We suggest taking grief recovery actions in regards to all three relationships. As you do so, the crying will diminish, and fond memories will not turn painful on you.

From our hearts to yours,
Russell and John

Feelings Don't Happen "Just Out of the Blue"

Corinne from MD writes:
My mama died a few months ago. I've had uncontrollable crying spells for twenty minutes at work, at home, and on dates in public places. Why, just out of the blue, does this happen? Is it normal to feel you failed after a parent dies, because you couldn't do more to prevent it?

Dear Corinne,
It's very common to have those kinds of uncontrollable crying jags, and to have them at times and in places where you'd rather feel more under control. So please understand that it's well within the range of normal and natural reactions to the death of someone important to you.

While it appears to "just happen out of the blue," it really doesn't happen that way. Even though you may not be consciously aware of it, some part of your brain and heart is focused on your mom and the fact that she's no longer alive.

Also, many people question themselves after someone has died, wondering whether they could have done more or been there more for the dying person. It's your broken heart that asks that question. As you've probably guessed, it's not a question that can really be answered, but we hope you'll be able to take the actions of grief recovery to help you become emotionally complete with all those things you wish you could have done *differently, better, or more.*

From our hearts to yours,
Russell and John

Very Attached to Their Possessions

Penelope from NC writes:
It has been almost eight months since my mother died. Her clothing still smells like her, and I'm telling you, it's hard for me to let go of her belongings. I'm not doing well reconnecting with my children. My four-year-old daughter asked if I miss her and when she asked if I cry she too lost a tear. Just typing this message is tearing me apart. Does it go away? What do I need to do?

Dear Penelope,
Let us first address the issue of your mother's belongings. Dealing with clothing and other possessions is often a very difficult and emotional task—so much so that we devote a section of our book to it.

On pages 162–164 of *The Grief Recovery Handbook*, there's a section called "Clean-up Work." It gives an excellent and practical plan for dealing with clothing and other possessions.

There's an alert at the top of page 163 which says, "When possible, never do any of these chores alone." That's an excellent piece of guidance. One of the things it does is to remind you that if you have someone there, you can talk about your mother. If you have an emotional reaction you'll have someone to be with you rather than being alone with those feelings.

There are three elements in the plan we wrote in the book. One is to identify all the things of your mom's that you definitely want to keep; another is to identify which things you definitely don't want or need; and a third group of things that you're not sure about. That last batch gets put in bags or boxes and stored in the garage. Six months later, you can take that batch out, go through it again, and create three more groups: keep, discard, and put in the garage. Over a year or a year and a half, you will have kept exactly what you really most want, and will have no regrets about what you've let go.

But possessions are only one piece of the equation. Based on what you said in your note, you probably would be well advised to take all the actions outlined in the *Handbook*. As you take the actions, you'll find yourself with less pain, fewer tears, and more fond memories of your relationship with your mom. You'll find that you can move forward in your life and not feel "torn up" just thinking or talking about her.

From our hearts to yours,
Russell and John

ROBBED OF GOODBYE: Q&A

Sudden Death Robs Us of a Last Goodbye

Jonathan from IL writes:
Back in February, my best friend was killed in a car accident. My heart is broken. I don't feel good about anything. When I do start to feel half-way good for a minute, it hits me again and I feel so sad. I almost seem to shake it, but it's tough because I keep wishing I had been able to say goodbye or something. The same thing happened with my dad, who died on the operating table. Never saying goodbye is so painful, so frustrating. I ask God to let me talk to her. Will it happen?

Dear Jonathan,
We're not surprised that you don't feel good about anything. After all, the sudden tragic death of your best friend has turned your universe upside down. What you describe about starting to feel halfway good, and then going down the elevator shaft, is a very common reaction. We call it a roller coaster of emotions. As painful as it is, it's a normal and natural reaction to what has happened—you're not crazy. What's really hard is the fact that you didn't get to say goodbye. That's almost always the case when there's been a sudden death—and in addition to losing the person, the feeling of being unfinished tends to stay with you.

As you might imagine, we can't really answer your sad question about being able to talk to her. We know it's your broken heart talking. We can direct you to *The Grief Recovery Handbook*, which you can get in the library or a bookstore. The purpose of the book is to help you discover and complete what the death left unfinished for you, including all the unrealized *hopes, dreams, and expectations* for the future and especially the missing goodbye.

From our hearts to yours,
Russell and John

No Longer Together, but Still Heartbroken

Mathilde from WV writes:
My heart aches. I just found out a friend that I dated died 5 months ago. I talked to him before he died, but he never gave me any indication that he was sick or moving out of town. When I called the number it was disconnected. My sister found his name on the Internet. I feel so hurt I did not get a chance to say goodbye, or pay my respects. How do I heal from this? I cry every day.

Dear Mathilde,
Sometimes the things we don't know are so difficult to deal with. We imagine it's almost impossible for you to understand why he didn't let you know that something was wrong with him or that he was planning to move away.

In grief recovery, we talk about all the things we wish had been *different, better, or more,* and this circumstance leaves you stuck with wondering what happened and why. The way he didn't communicate also robbed you of the chance to say goodbye, as well as other things you might have wanted to say to him.

The Grief Recovery Handbook outlines the actions you can take that will help you feel more emotionally complete with these things, and will guide you in saying goodbye and anything else you might need to communicate, even though it will obviously be an indirect communication.

From our hearts to yours,
Russell and John

Is There Such a Thing as Complicated Grief?

Carol from AR writes:
Is there such a thing as complicated grief for someone who was lost many years ago? We really never said goodbye prior to his death.

Dear Carol,
If you've read some of the Q&A we've posted on Tributes.com, you'll have noticed we don't use that phrase "complicated grief" or "complicated bereavement." That language is getting more and more common, but is not language we're comfortable with. We don't think there's any such thing as "complicated grief," though there are those who would disagree.

We believe all grief is experienced at 100 percent; there are no half-grievers, and anything that compares or ranks grief is incorrect and possibly dangerous to the griever. The phrase "complicated grief" is comparative from the outset as it indicates there must also be uncomplicated grief.

We also believe that if you don't address the unfinished emotional business that exists in all relationships—good, bad, and sometimes ugly—then what is incomplete stays unresolved. Since time can't heal emotional wounds, it only gets worse, not because it's complicated, but because it's not attended. The best way to understand it is to think of a cut finger. If you don't clean it, it can become infected, and you can have a real problem. The original cut was not "complicated"; it became compromised by lack of proper cleaning and care. The same is true for grief.

Now to your question about someone you didn't say goodbye to many years ago: What we say is that "unresolved grief is cumulative and cumulatively negative and since time can't heal emotional wounds, unattended grief can only get worse." Being robbed of the chance to say goodbye—if that was the circumstance—or if you chose not to say goodbye for other reasons can cause the undelivered emotional communication to be buried out of sight, and therefore remain incomplete.

It doesn't really get complicated—it just remains unfinished—and that can become a really big problem. When one or only a few elements of the relationship remain incomplete, it tends to keep the entire relationship unfinished. That's what might appear to be a complication, but it's really a lack of helpful action compounded over a long period of time.

The principles and actions of grief recovery are predicated on the idea that when someone dies, there will inevitably be some things we wish had been *different, better, or more*; and there will always be unrealized *hopes, dreams, and expectations* for the future. That's true in the best of relationships as well as the worst, and everything in between.

As you take the actions of grief recovery, you'll make many discoveries—other than just the missing goodbye—within your relationship with the person who died so long ago. The book will show you how to complete what was left unfinished, either unsaid or not done, in the most effective way possible.

From our hearts to yours,
Russell and John

When I Need Him One More Time, He's No Longer Here

Zara from HI writes:

How can I get over the death of my grandfather who raised me? He was the only father I ever really knew. After his death, I paid off a few of his debts with no help from his children. I even paid for his headstone but that doesn't really bother me because he was my father in every respect of the word.

At times I feel his presence. Sometimes, I just find myself crying at the thought of him. He left me his house, but to keep down confusion, I have decided to let his wife, my grandmother, take over. I'm trying very hard to deal with it, but sometimes, I just don't know how. He was ALWAYS there for me whenever I needed him.

I visit his gravesite very often but a friend of mine told me that it's not healthy and that I should just move on. The problem is, I don't know how. I think about him every day. And I mean, every day. I think what bothers me most is that I was on my way to the hospital when he died and I never really got a chance to say "goodbye." What am I suppose to do? I really don't know how to cope with this. It's been three years and I still am not able to cope with it. Help me, please!

Dear Zara,

Thanks for your note and questions. As we read them, our eyes (and hearts) focused in on the word ALWAYS, which you wrote in all capital letters. Without hesitation we knew we'd want to share with you a definition of grief we heard someone say many years ago:

"Grief is the feeling of reaching out for someone who has ALWAYS been there, only to find when I need him one more time, he is no longer here."

We write that phrase in all our books, and we tell the story that surrounds it in all of our lectures and workshops. We share it with everyone because it helps them realize that their own feelings of grief—of missing someone profoundly—are normal and natural and healthy. Hopefully, you will have the same awareness.

A great deal of what you wrote affected us immediately, especially, "He was the only father I really knew." We are not surprised that you have as much emotion as you do and that you miss him so much. With that in mind, it only makes sense that you think of him every day—no matter how many years have gone by.

The fact that you never got to say "goodbye" compounds the problem for you, and would come under the heading of "undelivered emotional communications," which represents *unresolved grief* rather than raw grief. In fact, one of the most common issues we've heard in our thirty-five years of helping grievers is the exact, painful sentence you used, "I never got a chance to say goodbye."

Again, we tell you that so that you'll realize how normal it is to feel robbed of the chance to say one last goodbye. The fact that you may have said goodbye to him thousands of times over the years—after each visit and at the end of every phone call—does not fill in the emotional blank left by not having one more and one last goodbye.

The good news is that the actions of grief recovery are dedicated to helping people "discover and complete" what was left emotionally unfinished for them at the time someone important to them died—and to help them with things they discover a long time after the death. That includes being able to say "goodbye" in a meaningful way.

As you take those actions, you'll sense a shift in how you feel. You'll be able to retain all the fond memories, but the pain and discomfort will subside. You'll stop replaying that trip to the hospital where you didn't make it in time. And if it's true that you've been hard on yourself for not getting there on time, you'll stop beating yourself up about it.

From our hearts to yours,
Russell and John

Relationships Are Made Up of Time and Intensity!

Carole from NM writes:
I only had the love of my life for a few months and I never got to say "I love you" or "goodbye." This pain is so bad I can't function. I want to get through this, but how do I and when will I be able to stop grieving?

Dear Carole,

Relationships are made up of both time and intensity. Some people may try to minimize your grief based on the relatively short length of the relationship, but when someone uses the phrase "love of my life," we know that means there was/is a great deal of emotional intensity attached to the relationship. Also, we believe that all grief or loss is experienced at 100 percent and that your heart is totally broken.

Compounding the pain of his death for you is the absence of one last "I love you" and "goodbye," even though if you'd had a chance to see him and say those things, you'd still be devastated. The Grief Recovery Method® actions will help you become emotionally complete with these things, which in turn will allow you to function in life.

Sadly, we can't bring him back, but the actions can help you get your heart back and allow the fond memories you have to go forward with you. As you do this, the grieving will subside, but you'll still have the capacity for sadness and joy about him, and about the other relationships you have with people in your life. The feeling we want to diminish is the pain.

From our hearts to yours,
Russell and John

Missing the Funeral

Margaret from AL writes:
How do I deal with the fact my sister waited two weeks to let me know that my niece had died and that they had the funeral the week before? I didn't get to say goodbye.

Dear Margaret,

This is a tough one. We'd have to guess that part of the problem is that there may be an ongoing issue between you and your sister, or that the two of you are not very close at all. Otherwise we can't imagine why she didn't tell you. On the other hand, your feelings of regret about not having been able to say goodbye to your niece indicate that you had a good relationship with her.

Regardless of the reasons, it's not possible to turn the clock back and attend the funeral with the stimulus of the casket, the ceremony, and the memories and stories people shared about your niece.

However, you might want to find out if anyone videotaped the memorial or funeral, and if so, see if you can get a copy. Although a video isn't the same as the actual service, you can hear what was said and get a sense of the emotions in the chapel, which may trigger some for you. It can also remind you of things you wish you'd said to her or done with her. Her death robbed you of the ability to say and do those things and, along with the missing goodbye, is part of why you feel robbed by not being notified so you could be there.

Another thing you can do is have your own memorial service. Hopefully you can find some other family members who'd want to spend some time sharing memories and stories of your niece. At the end of that occasion, you could say goodbye to a picture of her. Grief recovery actions can also help you get complete with the loss of your niece as well as any loss of trust you may have regarding your sister.

From our hearts to yours,
Russell and John

Cremains as a Permanent Relocatable Grief Recovery Monument

Tracey from NE writes:

It has been nearly 2 years since my mom died, but she left us with so many questions. We're told she overdosed on pills. Stories just don't match, don't make sense, and till this day bother me. Part of me acts as if she's still there, just not calling because she lives in another state. One of my sisters and I had to make funeral arrangements, though neither of us had a job. We raised the money to have her cremated and sent back home to us. Some say we're odd because we hold on to her ashes. We split her up between the sisters. Is this odd? Sometimes I touch the ashes and talk to her. I don't want her ashes gone. Many say I'm holding on. When you have the question of why, how do you overcome this? Those questions seem to hang on forever.

Dear Tracey,

Dealing with the death of someone important to us is painful and difficult enough without the addition of so much confusion when we don't know exactly what happened.

We want to focus on your heartfelt comments and questions about your mom's ashes. We believe that it's an excellent idea for each of you sisters to have a portion of the ashes. That way you can always have a sense of connection, not only to your mom, but to your family history.

Having the ashes in an urn in your own home becomes a "permanent relocatable grief recovery" place where your memories can be the most accurate about your relationship with your mom. And, as you indicate, you do just that when you touch the ashes and talk to her. That's perfectly normal and healthy.

The only thing we might suggest you add are some recovery actions that will help you become more emotionally complete in your relationship to your mom, and to the absence of information about her death.

The Grief Recovery Handbook spells out the actions you can take and, as you do, you'll find those constant questions which have been plaguing you for the past three years will disappear. They simply won't be as important after you've become emotionally complete with your mom.

From our hearts to yours,
Russell and John

OTHER TYPICAL, NORMAL, AND NATURAL RESPONSES TO LOSS: Q&A

Quieting the Inner Dialogue That Never Sleeps

Bettina from NV writes:
Both of my parents died a day apart. It's been over a year. I suffered other major losses two years before the deaths of my parents. Now I can find nothing but loss and death in my thoughts. How can I come back to the living? I can't stop that inner dialogue.

Dear Bettina,
You're so right. It can be torture to be unable to quiet those inner voices. This is especially true when you look in your life's rearview mirror and you only see the litany of losses that have happened over the past few years. We'd bet that other losses from your more distant past also crop up when that dialogue starts talking to you.

It would be too simple for us to just say that those voices are your "broken heart talking." Although we believe that's true, it doesn't fix anything and knowing that doesn't stop the noise.

The probable fact is that your broken heart is going over and over your individual relationships with each of your parents who died, and your relationships with the people and events two years prior. It just goes over the details, with emotions attached, but does nothing to help you complete what the deaths left emotionally incomplete for you. Therefore, all it can do is loop the story and go back over it again.

We strongly recommend that you go to the library or bookstore and get a copy of *The Grief Recovery Handbook*. Read it and take the actions it outlines. We believe it's the most effective and helpful way to quiet those voices without just trying to push them out of your mind by distracting yourself with louder noises, or burying them out of sight. As you can guess, if you push them out of sight, they will come back and haunt you later.

One more thing: It's common to feel overwhelmed when you have a long list of losses, especially when they are about your relationships with the most important people in your life. Since unresolved grief is cumulative and cumulatively negative, and since time can't heal emotional wounds, you'll have to take the actions of grief recovery on each of the major relationships affected. You can't do your parents as a group—they are each individual relationships. Get started on this as soon as possible.

From our hearts to yours,
Russell and John

Life Itself Just Seems Very Tasteless— Nothing Seems To Matter

Molly from OR writes:
My dad died a year ago and life hasn't been the same. Every morning I get up and wonder why he left us. I know it wasn't up to him to decide, but he was the best friend I ever had. Whenever I think about him, I see his hands reaching out to catch me whenever I fell.

Life itself just seems very tasteless—nothing seems to matter. Everything seems to end with that last breath he took. I can't go to my parents' house because every time I enter, every corner seems to tell a story of him. I feel like the person that cared for us the most is no longer here and no one else seems to care. How can I get back my love for life?

Dear Molly,
We reacted to your poignant language that "Life itself just seems very tasteless, nothing seems to matter." We know that millions of people can relate to what you've said. And although there's no need to redefine your words, we would like to comment on what you wrote in your note to us.

When someone important to us dies, the rest of the world goes out of focus. The things that are typically important to us recede into the background. The only thing that's important is the absence of that person, and the automatic review of the relationship we had with him or her. What we most want you to know is that what you report about your thoughts and feelings is totally normal and natural, and even healthy.

There's something else we'd like to share with you about what you're feeling. We once heard someone define grief this way, "Grief is the feeling of reaching out for someone who has always been there, only to discover, when I need him one more time, he is no longer there."

We also want to share with you the idea that "unresolved grief drains energy and robs choice." We can tell from the content and tone of your note, that both are true for you right now.

With those things in mind, we strongly recommend that you take the actions of grief recovery. It's the only emotionally helpful method we know of that can aid you in discovering and completing what's left unfinished for you. We have no doubt that as you take those actions, you will rediscover your will to live and participate fully in life once more, with fond memories of your dad firmly in your heart.

From our hearts to yours,
Russell and John

Inability to Concentrate Is an
Almost Universal Reaction

Steven from OK writes:
My friend was hit in her car one night three years ago and she died. Will the pain ever ease a little? She's all I can think of. It will probably affect my grades. Is there any way to help ease the pain?

Dear Steven,

We imagine that the sudden death of your friend has turned your world upside down. And with that, YES, your grades will probably be affected. The most common reaction to loss is an inability to concentrate. We suggest that you make your situation known to your teachers and, if necessary, request extensions for doing homework or taking tests. With that in mind, be gentle with yourself if you discover that you can't focus very well for now, and even for some time to come.

As for trying to ease the pain and when that might happen: Since everyone is a unique individual, it's impossible for us to guess how long the "raw" pain will affect you. We can tell you that rather than trying to fight it or avoid it, it's best to go with it. The pain you feel is the *normal and natural reaction* to the death of your friend. As your mind, your heart, and your body adapt to the new and unwanted reality, the pain will naturally subside.

However, the reduction of pain will not mean that you are emotionally complete with your friend who died. It will only mean that you are adapting to the loss.

Taking grief recovery actions will help you deal with the emotional incompleteness that is an automatic by-product of this sudden death. You'll find the pain diminishing, even though you'll still have sad feelings and miss your friend.

From our hearts to yours,
Russell and John

Still Hurt and Angry

Linda from ME writes:
My fiancé died two years ago. He was my "everything." It hurts as bad as it did when it first happened, but when I think of it I get extremely angry. Is this normal?

Dear Linda,
Based on what you wrote, we don't know what makes you angry—if it was primarily the fact that he died, or if it was the cause or circumstances of his death, or something else altogether. Without knowing specifically what provokes your anger, we can't give you a clear-cut response.

Whatever the cause, it's well within the range of normal to be angry, especially in the immediate aftermath. However, even though time can't heal emotional wounds, at this point two years on, the anger may no longer be normal and may have become an unhelpful habit that you're trapped in.

We do know that many people get so caught up in the cause of death that they stay angry with how it happened and never really get to do any kind of emotional recovery about the relationship that the death ended.

We also know that although anger is real, it's not usually the primary feeling we have when someone important to us dies. Anger is often an indirect expression of the fear we feel in those circumstances. Put into words, that fear might sound like this, "How do I go on without him?"

Based on what you wrote to us—"He was my everything"— we'd guess that it was a wonderful relationship and that you may very well be experiencing that sense of "How do I go on without him?" If that's true, we'd suggest that you shift from talking about anger and say, "I'm still feeling scared about my life and my future without him." Of course, you can still feel anger, but adding the truth about fear will be helpful.

Assuming the anger persists, regardless of what's causing it, you need to learn the actions that will help you become emotionally complete with all the now unrealizable *hopes, dreams, and expectations* for the future you had hoped to share with him. As you take the actions of recovery, you will find that the anger will disappear.

Please understand, we're not saying that doing the work we suggest will take away all of your sad or even angry feelings. Our goal for you is threefold. We want you to be able to have fond memories of him that do not turn painful. We want you to be able to remember him as you knew him in life, not death. And we want you to have a life of meaning and value even though he's not here.

From our hearts to yours,
Russell and John

Will I Ever Feel Normal Again?

Michael from DE writes:
Will I ever feel normal again?

Dear Michael,

Great question! We define grief as "the conflicting feelings caused by a change or an end in a familiar pattern of behavior." With that definition in mind, we certainly can relate to your question about ever feeling normal again.

The death of someone important to us changes everything that we've been familiar with and therefore everything we perceive as normal. After a death, things don't go back to the way they were, because things really are different. That means that what is normal will now be different. Adapting to life without someone here requires a new sense of what is normal. This happens to some degree as we learn to exist, day by day, without the other person. But time alone isn't all that's needed for us to feel okay about our new life and to begin to feel a new kind of normal.

If you've been reading some of the questions about grief and our answers on Tributes.com, you will have noticed that we almost always recommend that people get a copy of *The Grief Recovery Handbook* (available in most libraries and bookstores), read it, and take the actions it suggests. This is to help them discover and complete what was left emotionally unfinished by the death of someone important to them. Even though your note didn't indicate who had died, we know it had to have been someone who was meaningful in your life. So we guide you to the book and actions just like we do with others.

We can't bring the past back, but doing the reading and the work in the book can help you gain a new sense of normal in your life.

From our hearts to yours,
Russell and John

The Victims' Families Often Feel as if They Are on Trial

Anonymous from ID writes:
My husband was brutally murdered almost a year ago. We had a very strong, loving relationship and I don't feel I'm doing well at all. Is it possible that after all the court dates and trial, I will feel different, better? The murderer is in county jail awaiting trial. He has not even put in a plea yet. Right now, I feel like I could die from a broken heart.

Dear Anon,
Let us answer in two parts—first addressing the fact that you're embroiled in the court system. One of the most compounding emotional problems happens when grieving people are involved in legal proceedings. So let us say that our hearts go out to you beyond the pure grief you feel at your husband's death.

We know you most probably feel a need to be there to see justice done, but we also know that the constant stimulus in the courtroom is almost too much to bear, and keeps hammering home the fact that your husband died a violent death. We also know from all the people we've talked to that the families of the murdered people often feel they're on trial more than the perpetrator. To that end, we hope you have someone you trust who attends the court dates with you, and also that you have at least one person to debrief with every day so you can process the build-up of emotions that inevitably occurs.

Yes, we imagine it does feel like you could die of a broken heart. With that feeling, and the fact that emotions can indeed affect your health, please make sure you do the emotional debriefing we mentioned above as often as you can. In addition to this, taking grief recovery method actions is the best thing you can do to ensure that both your emotional and physical well-being are maintained. We'd guess you already realize that "when" the perpetrator is found guilty and punished, you'll still have a broken heart about the death of your husband. The sooner you do the grief recovery work, the better you'll be able to deal with the ongoing stimulus created by the trial.

From our hearts to yours,
Russell and John

The Emotional Pink Elephant in the Living Room

Jenny from VT writes:
My 28-year-old son died unexpectedly five years ago. Many people say I shouldn't be so emotional after this long, when I talk about him. His brother and father don't talk about him because it makes me emotional. I tell them they just need to give me a box of tissues, but we've never had a talk about him as a family since his death. Is this unusual?

Dear Jenny,

We agree, there can never be enough tissues. Over the years we've learned that grief is indeed unique and the pace at which people experience the emotions of grief bears a direct relationship to how they normally react emotionally to other life events.

We'd guess it's your nature and style to be open and emotive with your feelings, and it would be normal for you to still have feelings five years on, as it will be in ten or twenty years. If that's true, we say, YAY! This is a normal and natural response to the death of someone important to you as a unique individual.

Of course we're saddened by the nonactions of his brother and father. In not talking about him—even in their incorrect belief that they're protecting you from your own feelings—they rob you (and themselves) of sharing the very emotions that are helpful for you to feel and express. We don't say that to judge them but because we know that "grieving people need and want an opportunity to talk about what happened and their relationship with the person who died." Sadly, it's not unusual for families to avoid or ignore the emotional pink elephant in the living room.

While we'd love to encourage you to suggest to his brother and father that you have an evening of memories about the young man who meant a great deal to all of you, we don't know if they'd be at all receptive. The fact may be that the two men in question are apprehensive about their own emotions and are afraid to let it all out. If that's the case and they don't want to have the joy, sadness, and other feelings in relation to your son's life, then you need to look around your extended family for people who know you and knew your son who might be open to sharing stories and feelings about him.

From our hearts to yours,
Russell and John

Massive Reminders of Someone Who Is No Longer Alive

Anonymous from WV writes:
My husband died in 2007. I still can't sleep in our bed.

Dear Anon,

That's not unusual. Certain areas of a home, and particularly a bedroom or bed, are massive reminders of someone who's no longer alive. The stimulus of those places can make it seem almost impossible to be there or to relax when you are there. You have the obvious option of sleeping in a different room or a different bed, but the problem with that is that the unease and fear go with you and never go away.

Taking grief recovery actions will enable you to have fond memories of your husband without those memories turning painful for you and you'll probably be able to regain the ability to be in the bed and to deal with other difficult reminders you may have.

From our hearts to yours,
Russell and John

My Mom's Picture

Freya from TX writes:
When will I be able to look at my mom's picture again without crying and falling totally apart? I'm able to face most days without issue but now I'm also dealing with surgical menopause and cry almost nonstop about all things, especially about missing my mom. I really need help with my feelings and getting a true understanding of what I'm going through, and what is normal and expected when a parent dies.

Dear Freya,
The range of normal and natural emotions following the death of someone important to you is very wide. What you mention in your note definitely falls within that range. In fact, the issue of the emotional stimulus caused by pictures and other reminders is very typical and nothing to be overly concerned about. In addition, your impending surgery produces a ton of feelings about the changes it implies, not to mention the natural fears we all have about surgery, which are all within the range of normal.

Missing your mom, *especially at a time when you are scared and about to have surgery*, is about as normal as it gets. We assume that if your mom were alive she'd be the one you'd turn to with all your emotions and fears.

We don't know how long it's been since your mom died, and while we preach against the idea that "time heals all wounds," we're also very clear that in the first few weeks and months after the death of someone important to you, grief can be very raw and persistent, as in your statement, "[I] cry almost nonstop about all things . . ."

No matter what, we strongly recommend that you go to the library or bookstore and get a copy of *The Grief Recovery Handbook*. As you read it and take the actions it outlines, you'll sense a shift relative to the issues mentioned in your note and you should be able to look at pictures of your mom and have fond memories, even if there is some sadness attached.

From our hearts to yours,
Russell and John

Why Do Families Tear Apart?

Amy from KY writes:
Why do families tear apart when a parent is dying? How can siblings avoid, ignore, or cause so much trouble when the parent was so incredible and involved in family gatherings?

Dear Amy,
Great question! Why do people behave the way they do—especially in a real life and death crisis? If we could give a perfect answer to this question, we'd understand the secret of the universe. Here's what our experience indicates: There are two sets of relationship issues within a family when someone is dying:

1. The individual and unique relationship each person has with the dying person, and

2. The individual and unique relationships each person has with the other family members.

Some of those relationships may be good, some may be bad, and many will be a mixture of the two. Some will even be ugly. Add that all together and you have a recipe for emotional disaster, with the possibility of some pretty poor behavior.

Another major element is money or property. We can't tell you the kinds of stories we've heard about issues of money and property—stories that make you question the virtue of human morality or behavior.

The money or property issues offer the clearest explanation of the problem, but the driving force behind everyone's behavior is "fear." Fear, in this sense, is neither rational nor logical.

Fear is about losing something we have or not getting something we want. When it comes to money, property, and possessions, we've all seen other people behave badly—and some of us may have been guilty of that as well.

Fear dominates because the death of someone meaningful in our lives generates a tremendous amount of emotion. A great deal of that feeling is the result of the almost automatic review we make about our relationship with the dying person when we learn that their life is under siege, and as the dying process unfolds. Whether the relationship has been good, poor, or mixed, that review causes us to think about all the things we wish had been *different, better, or more* and about all *hopes, dreams, and expectations* for the future that will now go unrealized.

Because most people don't know how to deal effectively with the things that fall under the headings of *"different, better, or more"* and *"hopes, dreams, and expectations,"* they get scared. As we said, fear is neither rational nor logical and it isn't pretty.

We realize as we write this note to you, at best, you will have more of an understanding about why this happens, but it won't fix anything and it won't necessarily make you feel any better about what has happened and what you've seen with your family.

The one thing we might suggest is that you forgive the members of your family who you believe have acted poorly. Keep in mind that forgiveness is a private action—one that you take to relieve yourself of the uncomfortable feelings you have about others. Please don't forgive any of your people directly, either in person or by mail, email, phone, etc.

While you're holding on to any resentment you feel about the others, you remove yourself from the primary issues of your grief about your parent who died. Take the action of the indirect forgiveness of the people who trouble you so that you can stay focused on the incredible person who meant so much to you.

From our hearts to yours,
Russell and John

PART THREE

A Host of Questions on Unique Situations

Chronicling Dates
Painful Images
Guilt and Blame
Being Ruled from the Grave
Adults with Childhood Losses
Avoiding Certain Metaphors When Talking to Children about Grief
And More

The following chapters contain many questions on topics that you may relate to from your own experience. In addition to giving you answers to questions that may have occurred to you at some time, you'll learn ways you can listen to and talk with friends or family who are being affected by similar issues.

CHAPTER
ELEVEN

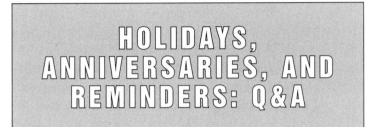

HOLIDAYS, ANNIVERSARIES, AND REMINDERS: Q&A

Today Is Way Too Long to Stay Stuck in One Feeling

Barbara from OH writes:
The love of my life died two days before Christmas. It was a very sad and emotional time in my life, to watch the man I love so much die in front of my eyes; the feeling of being so helpless, knowing that it was God's wish to take him home. Now it's the first Valentine's Day alone since he died and the feeling I have today is so empty and alone. I miss him so much, even though we were only married a short time. We shared every waking moment we had together and that's what I find so hard today, the empty feeling and the loneliness. What can I do to help the grieving?

Dear Barbara,
Valentine's Day is a chronicling date that has extra meaning when a spouse has died. Your grieving needs no help. The thoughts and feelings you mentioned in your note are normal and natural reactions attached to the death of your spouse, especially related to the major holidays couples share.

One of the problems for you is that he was probably the person you went to for comfort when your heart was sad, and now his death is the cause of your sadness, but you can't go to him for comfort.

One thing you can do is make sure you have a few safe people to whom you can express your feelings in the moment you're having them. When talking about how you feel, keep it as simple as possible. Avoid long stories about your pain if you can.

Here's a tip: When you have a feeling of sadness, loneliness, etc., say to one of your trusted people, "In this moment, I feel very sad," or very alone, or whatever you feel. That way, that moment can pass, and you can go to the next moment. Say, "In this moment," instead of saying, "Today I feel." Today is too long to stay stuck in one feeling.

While your loss is very raw and new, it's to be expected that your feelings and energy will be low and that concentration will be difficult. Accept those natural facts and allow yourself to feel and express the feelings you're having.

Once you begin to shift from grief to taking grief recovery actions, you'll learn to deal with the emotions you're experiencing. Grief recovery actions will also help you to become as emotionally complete as possible with what happened with your mate's death as well as with the loss of the *hopes, dreams, and expectations* you had for your future together.

From our hearts to yours,
Russell and John

Multiple Deaths Make Us Feel Like We're Drowning

Rebecca from IN writes:
This is the second Christmas, but it's only been a year and a half since my mother died. My sister died two years ago and my brother died this past fall. The holidays are getting harder and it's probably because I've lost so many people in a small amount of time. I've known I was depressed this season. I barely celebrated and that was because I moved into a friend's basement, with her and her family upstairs. This holiday season at work has been hard. Several parents or siblings of co-workers have died, which reminds me of my losses. How do I start feeling a little better? How do I start moving on?

Dear Rebecca,

When there are several deaths of people who are important to us, one after the other after the other, it can feel like we're drowning, and every time we start to get our heads above water, another wave comes and pushes us down.

It can be truly overwhelming all by itself, but it's compounded when we don't know what to do to become emotionally complete with each of the relationships we had with the people who died. Just as the losses happened one at a time, your recovery actions must be one loss at a time.

Grief recovery will help you discover and complete what was left emotionally unfinished for you in each of your relationships with the people who died, and that's what will help you start feeling a little better and be able to move forward and start participating more fully in your life again.

From our hearts to yours,
Russell and John

The Holidays—A Perfect Time to Demonstrate the Truth to Your Children

Cathy from AR writes:

My father died in August. He loved Thanksgiving more than any other holiday and made it very special for all of us. This is the first Thanksgiving without him and it's been very difficult for my family during this normally joyous time. I'm married with three children and I'm trying my hardest to put on a happy face for my family but, behind the smile, I'm very sad and somewhat depressed. I don't know how to get through this tough time without feeling this way.

Dear Cathy,

The first holiday after the death of someone important to you is almost always difficult. The natural pain you're having is compounded by the automatic reminders the holiday season carries about family and friends, and in many cases, the empty seat at the holiday dinner table.

We can relate to the power of the holidays. Russell's mother died the day before Thanksgiving nineteen years ago. Thanksgiving dinner the year after she died was awkward for him—and his dad and siblings. Over the following years, the pang of the holiday has lessened, but Thanksgiving for Russell is never without emotions related to the absence of his mother.

We want to focus on your statement, "I am trying my hardest to put on a happy face for my family . . ." Respectfully, we'd recommend that rather than putting on a "happy face," you put on an "honest face." When you cover up how you really feel and pretend to be okay, you'll really confuse your children. If they're very young, they won't understand why what they sense from your body language doesn't match what you are putting forward. Even if they're not very little, they rely much more on nonverbal communication than on words or ideas.

Keep in mind that as a parent you've always taught your children to "tell the truth" and now you're lying about how you feel. Their ability to trust you will be negatively affected if your communications don't match. It's perfectly healthy for them to see you being sad, and to hear you say that you're sad. You can then tell them the truth, with tears and other emotions attached. You can say, "I'm so sad. I miss my mommy—your grandma—so much. My heart hurts and my eyes fill up with tears." As you do this, you will teach them open, honest, and human ways to deal with and express their feelings. As parents we are always teachers, and that's what good teachers do.

One caution: We don't want any of your children to become your caretaker or therapist or surrogate parent or spouse. So even though you can be honest, you need to gently discourage them from taking care of you. Yes, it's a little delicate to do both, but you'll be able to figure out how to do that.

The Grief Recovery Handbook will be very helpful for you when dealing with your own loss, and *When Children Grieve* will help you guide your children through their grief without letting them become your caretakers.

From our hearts to yours,
Russell and John

It Is the Fact That He Died That Is Most Important, Not the Method or the Date

Janice from FL writes:

How do you get over hating Valentine's Day? That is the day I married the man with whom I shared my journey through life, and had a family with. That's also the day he killed himself, leaving me with two kids to take care of and heartache after heartache thereafter.

Dear Janice,

Important dates like holidays can definitely add emotions to the grief we already feel when someone important to us dies. When the death is a suicide, the emotional stakes go up exponentially. One of the problems with those two compounding factors is that they tend to distract you from the primary issue which is the *fact* that he died, not how or when he died. In fairness to you, based on having heard this kind of story from so many people, we imagine that it's difficult, if not impossible, *not* to focus on the suicide or the date.

We'd guess you believe he chose that date intentionally, and that just pounds another stake into your heart.

Our job is to gently and lovingly pry you off of the suicide and the date, and suggest that you consider your whole relationship with the man you shared your life with, not just the end of that journey.

If you stay focused on how he died rather than the fact that he died, you will let the cause of death overshadow the real issue which, again, is your relationship with him.

The same is true relative to Valentine's Day. While there may always be some emotion attached to that day for you, the key for you has less to do with that date than with becoming emotionally complete with your husband who died.

Even with the little bit we can gather from your note and question, and your powerful statement about being left with "heartache after heartache thereafter," we sense there may have been some struggles in the relationship.

It's painfully clear to us that you need to learn what will help you deal with your own broken heart so you can take care of and guide your children in their grief as well as in their lives.

Make sure you get copies of both *The Grief Recovery Handbook* and *When Children Grieve*. As you take grief recovery actions, you'll find both the date and the suicide assuming less importance than all the things that were part of your relationship with him.

From our hearts to yours,
Russell and John

Resetting the Dysfunctional Default Settings to Create a Fuller Life

Samantha from TX writes:
My mom died last year. This is the first Mother's Day that I don't have her. Why is it so hard and painful for me? I have no other family—she was all I had, but our relationship could best be described as dysfunctional.

Dear Samantha,
It's hard and painful for a lot of reasons.

1. In spite of whatever level of dysfunction, *she was your mother.*
2. As you say, you have no other family—she was all you had.
3. Holidays, with all the images of family connections, are very difficult, especially the first ones following a death.
4. Her death robs you of the possibility of repair of the dysfunction and the hope that it could have been replaced by warm feelings.
5. It's normal and natural to miss someone at times like holidays, even if the relationship could have been different and better.

Those are just a few reasons.

If you haven't taken any actions of grief recovery, you're simply looping the pain over and over and it doesn't get better. Without taking any actions to help you discover and complete what remains emotionally unfinished for you due to the dysfunction you mention, you can get stuck in that loop. It's essential that you take actions to help you break the cycle of pain that we imagine keeps reigniting the dysfunction that has affected much of your life. As you become emotionally complete with your mother who died, you'll find yourself able to create new habits and new positive functioning abilities as you move forward in your life.

From our hearts to yours,
Russell and John

Things That Don't Get to Happen Because They're No Longer Here

Annie from NH writes:
My father died two years ago. I'm still having trouble facing the fact that he's gone. I'll be graduating from high school this year. Is it normal to feel like I need him to be there or is that being selfish?

Dear Annie,

It's totally NORMAL to want your father to be at your high school graduation. In fact, as you probably have experienced over the past couple of years, it's at special events or special times that you become extra-aware of his absence and miss him. Holidays and birthdays are some of those events; and at your age, things like recitals or sports or other activities you participate in that he would normally attend can be extremely emotional because he isn't here to share them.

It's never selfish to need and want someone to be there in your life—particularly a parent when something important is going on for you.

There's a special section in *The Grief Recovery Handbook* from pages 174–178 which explains how to deal with the death of a parent when you are young, and how to deal with all the things that don't get to happen because they're no longer here.

From our hearts to yours,
Russell and John

Many Grieving People Struggle with Enjoying Themselves

Ginger from MT writes:
This will be the first holiday season without my husband. We were together for 45 years. Should I go to my family's Thanksgiving dinner, and my family's Christmas party? I feel guilty enjoying myself. Thank you.

Dear Ginger,

In the first year after the death of someone important to them, many grieving people struggle with enjoying themselves, being happy, laughing at jokes. The fact is that it's sad enough to be missing your spouse, the empty house, and all the places in the community that you went to together.

The amount of pain you feel and the amount of possible happy events you avoid do not indicate how much you loved him and miss him. If you tell us that you loved him and miss him, we believe you. And then if you laugh while remembering one of the cute or funny things he used to do, we'll laugh with you and enjoy your memories. And if you cry when talking about him, even in a happy way, we may get tears in our eyes because we are human too.

Please keep in mind that the forty-five years you had together contained a great deal of laughter and joy, and a certain amount of sadness and pain and frustration. So if your relationship with him in life included a wide range of emotions, why shouldn't your relationship to him after he has died also include all those feelings—happy, sad, the whole gamut?

It's your choice whether or not you go to family outings this holiday season. Based on what we've written, you already know our opinion. But keep in mind that if you're among people you know and hopefully trust, you'll be able to laugh and cry and participate in those holiday events. We hope you and the others toast your husband and all the other people who are no longer here.

From our hearts to yours,
Russell and John

Response from Ginger:
Dear Russell and John,

I was surprised to get your response and I'm so grateful to receive your advice. Everything you said is just the way I actually feel but this guilt keeps getting in my way. You're right, this guilt is stopping me from having a happy and joyous life and my husband would not want me to live this way. So I have decided to participate in my family's holiday parties and enjoy myself. I will call them and say, "I will be there, what time do we eat?" God's blessings to both of you and you are doing a good thing here. You have touched my life and made a difference. Thank you.

Will I Ever Be Able to Stop Being Numb and Let Go?

Cheryl from AK writes:
My dad died suddenly last year. My birthday was three days later. He was only 49 years old. Will I ever be able to stop being numb and let go? I still think every day that it was a bad dream and wait by the phone for him to call me. Does the loss of a parent ever become bearable? By the way I'm only 20.

Dear Cheryl,

Birthdays are important events in our lives and our parents are usually the first people we associate with those special days. Therefore, your dad's death falling so close to your birthday adds tremendous emotional impact to both events.

The sense of numbness will probably subside, but be alert to the fact that when the "emotional Novocain" wears off, there is sometimes a feeling of more pain, not less. You will have to adapt to that, but being aware of it may help you not to be surprised or too alarmed. It's part of the normal and natural reactions to the death of someone important to us.

When there's been a sudden death, it's not uncommon to have the feeling that it was all a bad dream—again that's a normal and natural reaction, and there's nothing wrong with the feelings and thoughts you're having. It's the way our broken hearts communicate to us about how difficult it is to adapt to this new, painful, unwanted reality.

The fact is you'll never forget your father and, to varying degrees, you'll probably always miss him. I can tell you something personal that may give you hope. Although I was substantially older than you are when my mother died suddenly nineteen years ago, I can still imagine everything she would have told me if and when I went to her for help or guidance. So even though

I lost her physically, I carry her with me emotionally and spiritually.

The key to making sure that you retain the positive and helpful aspects of the relationship—as I did with my mother—and to increasing your ability to adapt to your dad's death is to take the actions detailed in *The Grief Recovery Handbook*. If you need additional guidance as you work through the *Handbook*, please feel free to contact us.

From our hearts to yours,
Russell and John

CHAPTER
TWELVE

STUCK ON A PAINFUL IMAGE: Q&A

Staying Stuck on a Painful Image Keeps Us Stuck in Grief

Francis from SD writes:
My husband died just last year after I tried with all my might to breathe air into his asthmatic lungs. I watched as he choked and looked up and rolled his eyes. I tried and tried but I couldn't revive him! Now I have that image in my head of his struggling for air. Over and over it plays. My stepfather and father-in-law also died within several months of my husband's death. The grief is so heavy. I don't know what I should do. I've kept all my daily routines, working still, but nothing helps me with the heavy grief, crying, and the image of his not being able to breathe.

Dear Francis,

The issue of a recurring, painful last image or images of someone who has died is sadly common for many grieving people. In addition to the pain those images evoke, they often make us afraid to think about and remember the person we loved because it seems as if the only thing we can think of is that last terrible image.

It's a problem that happens for a great many people, which is why we wrote about it in *The Grief Recovery Handbook* (pages 157–158). We found that when people are stuck on those images, they have a hard time doing the work of grief recovery which will help them adapt to their changed lives. When you read those pages, you'll be able to reduce the dominating impact those images have on you. That will give you the freedom to take the actions of recovery outlined in the *Handbook*.

One of the results of taking the actions of recovery will be a reduction in that sense of heaviness of grief you've been feeling. You will also be able to remember your husband as you knew him in life, not only as you knew him in death.

From our hearts to yours,
Russell and John

Tragic Deaths Compound Our Pain

Anonymous from FL writes:
My father died tragically a few months ago. I was a witness to the
crime. I'm struggling. I put up a good front to others but on the inside
I'm barely making it. I cry every day. It's hard for me to talk about him.
I don't want anyone else to talk about him because it makes me sad. I
shy away from my daughter when she brings him up. I know that he's
gone, but for some reason, I'm having a very hard time accepting it. I
often feel that this is a dream and I will wake up. I miss him so much.
I need help.

Dear Anon,

While the "tragedy" aspect of your father's death may be dominating your heart and mind, the bottom-line truth may be that
your heart would be equally broken had he died in a different—
and perhaps more natural—way. Over the years we've seen people
get so caught up in *how* the death happened that they sometimes
lose sight of the fact that the death itself is what has broken their
heart rather than the cause of the death.

The other thing from your note we want to address is your
comment—"I don't want anyone to talk about him because it
makes me sad." Sad is the normal, healthy emotional reaction to
grief and, rather than moving away from it, you should move towards it. Rather than robbing yourself and your daughter of the
natural emotions of grief, share them. You might be surprised
that in talking and crying openly you'll find the pain diminishing
and memories of him and your relationship with him become
easier and more heartwarming to talk about.

As for your having a hard time accepting his death and your
feeling that it's a dream, these are also very common feelings
and thoughts and represent your broken heart that misses him
so much. It's not an uncommon reaction to find it difficult to

adapt to a death when there has been a tragic event, in particular a "sudden death" for which we're unprepared.

From our hearts to yours,
Russell and John

Trying "Not" to Think about It Doesn't Work

Eric from NY writes:
How do you try to get past what the person you loved did to end their life?

Dear Eric,

In one short sentence you have posed a most powerful question. It's a question that must be restated in order to answer it. "Getting past," like "getting over," carries the idea that you might somehow be able to forget what they did. That's not really possible.

Many people get stuck on the images attached to the end of someone's life. Whether it was cancer, an auto accident, or a murder, the images are sometimes very ugly. Certain methods of suicide are horrible to see or even think about. As you've probably already figured out, trying "not" to think about it doesn't work. What usually happens is that people just keep thinking about that ugly ending over and over and over. The problem, when you're stuck on the ending, is that you eliminate all of the other memories of the relationship you had with the person over your lifetime.

We teach people to acknowledge the pain of the last image and then think about and talk about some of the other things that they remember about their relationship with the person.

For example: We'll assume that the person who died was your spouse. If you told us how she took her life, we might say to you, "What a painful last image for you to have to carry forward." Then we would ask, "Can you remember the first time you ever saw her in your life?" What follows can be a conversation which allows you to access the entire relationship, not just the end of it. Then you can do the emotional work you need to do to deal with your broken heart.

From our hearts to yours,
Russell and John

Completion, Not Closure—
An Important Distinction

Samantha from MN writes:
My grandfather was like my father. I basically had to watch him die in front of my eyes in the hospital in less than two hours. It happened so fast that I still cry every other day and find it hard to find closure. How do I find closure and find a way to take this as a step to get stronger?

Dear Samantha,
Even though your note is short, there are a few different elements to it. First, the fact that your relationship with your grandfather was more like that with a father is very important. It means there's a lifetime of events with emotions attached that affected you, not just the circumstances and speed of his death. Many people get focused on the end of the relationship and lose sight of the whole relationship. As you take grief recovery actions, you'll find yourself feeling more and more emotionally complete with your grandfather. With that, you will be able to remember and think about the entire relationship and not just the ending.

Another element is the word-idea, "closure." When you read *The Grief Recovery Handbook,* you'll notice that the word closure only appears on page 18 when we say, *"Closure* is another unhelpful and inaccurate word." In part it's because we think closure implies something that is both incorrect and scary for people. That is, that closure implies the end of the relationship. When someone important to us dies, the aspect of the relationship that has ended is the physical one—the emotional and spiritual aspects continue as long as we're alive.

Rather than closure, we prefer to say that grief recovery helps people become "emotionally complete" with the things they wish had happened *differently, better, or more*, and with all the unrealized *hopes, dreams, and expectations* for the future.

From our hearts to yours,
Russell and John

Grief Is Not PTSD

Anonymous from TN writes:
I watched cancer take my brother nine months ago at the young age of
43. It hit without warning and four months later he was gone. I was
with him through it all and when he took his last breath. I still cry
every time I think of him. I'm not the same person I was. Could I have
PTSD? It just doesn't seem like he can really be gone. How can I work
through this?

Dear Anon,
We'd imagine that some of the images associated with your
brother's illness and death—not to mention his age and the speed
at which it happened—continue to recur in living color in your
mind and heart.

We're not doctors or therapists, but we don't think you have
PTSD. We know that diagnosis gets tossed around a lot but if it's
not accurate for you, it can really limit you. We do believe that
you're a griever with a broken heart. We also believe that the
circumstances of your brother's death, coupled with what we'd
guess was a very powerful relationship for you, keep you feeling
stuck with a boatload of emotions and that you have no sense of
how to get out from under so much feeling.

Assuming that we're correct, the first thing we want to say
is that your grief—even several months on—is normal and natural. Your broken heart does not need to be pathologized with a
diagnosis of PTSD or any other condition. Since your brother's
untimely death robbed you (and him) of the *hopes, dreams, and
expectations* for your futures together, a large part of what we
might term your "unresolved grief" relates to that future that
will not get to happen.

As you take the actions of grief recovery, you'll find the pain
diminishing and the bouts of crying reducing. At the same time,

you'll have a positive sense of retaining the fond memories you have of your relationship with your brother.

From our hearts to yours,
Russell and John

We Know What They Would Have Said

Jill from NV writes:
Why do I relive the day my mom died over and over again? It's been 5 years and it seems like just a few months ago. I still look at her picture (when she was ill) and cry. If I hear a sad song I still cry. We were extremely close.

Dear Jill,
Based on the comments you made, we'd guess that the person you would normally go to when your heart felt sad was your mom. With your mom's death, your sadness level probably went up as high as it could go, and she's the person you'd most want to talk to when you felt sad.

The fact is that many people—if not most—have ongoing emotional and spiritual relationships with important people to them who have died. And many people are comforted by the sense of connection they have with that person. They often have conversations with them. Even though they are one-way talks, we can imagine what Mom or Dad would have said back to us in most situations.

What we're saying is that it's normal to remember people and look at their pictures, and from time to time to be sad and miss them. However, if those things are dominating your life and not allowing you to move forward, then you probably need to take some actions to help you feel more emotionally complete with your mom's death. Taking grief recovery actions will help you start to feel a shift. Hopefully, that reliving of her last day will diminish, as will the pain and sadness that seem to be your constant companions.

From our hearts to yours,
Russell and John

As She Was Dying, My Mother Shut Me Out

Miranda from OH writes:
My mother died five months ago and I just don't feel like I'll ever be able to move past this. This pain is so great. I'm angry because she shut down before she died and blocked me out. We had a great relationship full of love. I just wanted her to say something. I no longer felt like her daughter. Was this her way of transitioning? Why am I so angry?

Dear Miranda,

Sadly, it's not uncommon for dying people to shut the most important people out of their lives, and it's most typical for a parent to do that to a child—even an adult child.

Why? Most of the time it's because the parent somehow thinks they are protecting the child by not letting them see them die. Or, even if they let the child visit, they don't talk openly and honestly about what they're experiencing, which has the impact of making the child feel even worse than they already do. It was very sad for us to read what you said about no longer feeling like your mother's daughter.

We'd guess that your anger is the direct and logical reaction to what your mother did that robbed you of the communication you wanted and needed. The real question is what can you do about it, now that she has died? A part of the answer is to be able to look at the whole relationship and not just the ending when she got sick and started withholding herself from you.

If you take the actions of grief recovery, you'll have a chance to review your whole life with your mother, and not just go over and over the things that happened near the end of her life. As you do that, the anger should subside, and you'll be able to be more focused on the primary fact that for most of your life, it was a great relationship. The book will also help you deal with the things that she did that kept you away from her, and you will once more be able to feel like her daughter.

From our hearts to yours,
Russell and John

I Know There's Nothing I Could've Done to Stop Him

Anonymous from MS writes:
My friend committed suicide, and I know there's nothing I could've done to stop him, but I really miss him. I just keep replaying it over and over in my mind. Help, please!

Dear Anon,

Missing your friend is the most normal and natural reaction to his death. Although grieving people often get stuck on a painful last image based on the way someone died, we believe you'd miss him just as much had he died some other way. So please don't let the fact that he died by suicide confuse you and keep you from moving towards recovery.

We're encouraged by your recognition that there was nothing you could have done. Many people get stuck thinking they could or should have known, or that they somehow could have stopped it from happening. As you already know, this is painful enough without adding a whole other idea that you could've done something.

The key for you is to learn how to discover and complete what was left emotionally unfinished for you with his death. We hope you'll go to the library or bookstore and get a copy of *The Grief Recovery Handbook*. As you read it and take the actions it outlines, you'll find a shift in how you feel. The pain should subside, but you'll be able to keep the fond memories of the friendship.

From our hearts to yours,
Russell and John

CHAPTER
THIRTEEN

GUILT AND BLAME: Q&A

The "Story-Line" Sometimes Trumps the "Heart-Line"

Jane from WI writes:
My husband of twenty years died unexpectedly ten weeks ago today. He was only forty-five, the love of my life, and my best friend. He was due to be released from the hospital when something happened. There was an inaccurate reading of his tests, his fatal condition was overlooked, and he died the next day. It's difficult enough just losing him. My son and I are having a terrible time coping with the loss and the anger from this "mistake" that led to his death. What do we do to get past the anger? We grieve and then we're hurt and angry . . . it's an emotional roller coaster. Why do I still feel in the back of my mind that I can have someone "fix it"? To call it an error or mistake is offensive to me—you can fix errors and mistakes usually. I'm an adult and can't filter all these emotions, so I'm extremely worried about my 12-year-old son.

Dear Jane,
As you already know, there are no words that can adequately address what's affecting you and your son. The major issues confronting you are the fact that your very young husband died, compounded by the tragic circumstances in which he died, and what we assume to be the less-than-sensitive communication about it from the doctors and hospital personnel.

As important as the circumstances of his death are to you and how much they affect you emotionally, the primary issue for you is your twenty-year relationship with him, and all the things that did and didn't happen during those years, as well as the future you and your son are robbed of.

The pull back to "how he died" and how you were treated that keeps tugging at you may be taking you away from your relationship with him and keeping you focused on the doctors, hospital, etc. Your anger at the "mistake" is normal, natural, and understandable, but you cannot let your anger at the hospital and the personnel involved rob you of your primary issue, your relationship with your husband.

We've seen people spend decades focused on the causes and circumstances of a death, and leave their person who died totally out of the equation. You must not let that happen to you—or to your son. None of this is to excuse, defend, justify, or otherwise minimize the horrific and gross fatal error made by the hospital and their personnel. That's inexcusable—period.

We're constantly called on to help people who find themselves in situations parallel to the one you're in, where the "story-line" of the death sometimes seems to trump the "heart-line" of the relationship with the person who died.

The hardest part of this note is to tell you that the first thing you must do, you may find difficult or even offensive. You must forgive the person(s) and the hospital that made the outrageous errors that led to your husband's death, otherwise you will continue to be drawn back to how he died rather than to your broken heart over the fact that he died. If you don't forgive them, you give your emotional power away to people and organizations that don't deserve it; and you keep yourself more focused on them than on your husband.

Forgiveness is the most difficult, least well understood, and least well-taught topic in our society. In *The Grief Recovery Handbook*, you will find the concept and actions of forgiveness explained in ways you've never seen before, and you will find it very helpful.

Here's a tip, even in advance of your reading more about the topic: Even if you struggle with forgiveness, you can add a few words that help you understand who the forgiveness is for. The words are, "I forgive you so that *I can be free*." In your situation, it will free you to do the really important work of becoming emotionally complete with your husband who died.

In the book, we distinguish between "forgive" and "condone" since so many people misinterpret forgiveness to mean that it's okay that someone hurt them or someone they love. We never excuse or condone bad, illegal, or immoral behavior, but we know that without forgiveness we carry forward the hurt we feel and re-wound ourselves over and over.

All the above is a preamble to your very heartfelt and legitimate concern about your son. Your son will be observing you and relying on what he sees and hears from you to help him learn what he needs to do to deal with his own broken heart. You are still his leader and—especially now that his other leader, his dad, has died—he will look to you for guidance. Since he's a teenager, he may not be polite and open in asking for your guidance but trust us when we tell you that he will be watching you.

The more you do to deal with your broken heart, and therefore the more and better you adapt to this horrific situation, the more your son will want to copy you.

Important within all this is that you not allow him to be your caretaker. It's a dangerous and incorrect position for him, and one for which he is not qualified. *The Grief Recovery Handbook* will be a guide for you in the actions of grief recovery. *When Children Grieve*, our other book, will help you guide your son.

We also wanted to comment on this part of your note: "I'm an adult and can't filter all these emotions." We want to acknowledge the honesty and accuracy of that statement. When your heart is broken your head doesn't work right, and when your heart is broken, your spirit cannot soar. We believe that if you get correct and helpful information for dealing with your own broken heart and your son's as well, you will be able to deal as effectively as possible with what is an impossible situation.

From our hearts to yours,
Russell and John

But for One Second Earlier or Later, Our Lives Are Changed Forever

John from OK writes:

Just over five months ago a drunk driver killed my stepfather of thirty-five years. It was my first day at a new job and I'd been driving an old family hand-me-down truck that had seen much better days. Throughout the day I made some conscious decisions regarding the use of the truck, knowing I might need to call my dad to get me out of yet another jam. To make a long story short, after helping me get the truck running, my dad was following me home. A drunk driver struck him head-on and he died in a matter of minutes. I drive this road twice a day, to and from work. Knowing in my heart what went on in my head that day makes everything so incredibly hard to deal with. People say that it was just his time—that he was doing what he always did. But I don't see it like that in any light. I can't see past the only reason he was on that road. I feel like it's easier to say when you don't expect the blame.

Dear John,

As a stepdad myself, I am very touched by your letter. And, like most people, I have gone over events in my life—including auto accidents—and realized that if I had left the house one second later or one second earlier, the accident probably wouldn't have happened. By the same token, I realized that in similar ways, I might not have met my spouse or gotten my job if a certain incredible string of things hadn't occurred. Even so, we all naturally do that kind of thinking after the fact, especially when something tragic has happened.

I think the biggest issue for you now is something that we have written about in previous responses to questions and which we address in one of our articles entitled *Stuck on a Painful Image* (reprinted on page 254). We think if you stay focused on the story and images of how your stepfather died, you're removed from the other really important issues, which are about your relationship with him and what he meant to you—and how much you meant to him.

I'm not a fan of the idea that "it was just his time" because even if that's somehow intellectually true, it's of no emotional value to you as a griever. I do believe your heart is broken in a million pieces and that you're not to blame for what happened. I also believe that grief recovery actions can help you stop blaming yourself and enable you to remember and talk about the whole relationship, not just the ending. They can also help you deal with whatever feelings you might still have about the drunk driver.

From our hearts to yours,
Russell and John

How Do I Accept the Things I Did?

Olivia from OR writes:
My grandma died in October. She raised me almost my whole life. I left home at around 17 and I came back to see her every once and a while. I knew she loved me and wanted me so badly in her life again. The week I moved back, my dad told me to go see her. I told him I would, but I had things to do for unpacking, and taking care of my son. A few days later I got a call from my dad saying grandma had died. I kick myself every day that I didn't visit her when I should have.

My dad and I were the only family grandma had here in Oregon, and she was the only thing my dad really had. When her funeral came around I never really, truly grieved. I was trying to be strong for my dad and my son. Now I can't stop thinking about her. Almost every day something reminds me of her. Every day I cry. I miss her so much. I pray every night, talking to her. I have a picture of her in my truck that I say is my guardian angel. Will I ever be able to accept this? How do I accept the things I did?

Dear Olivia,
Over the years we've gotten thousands of calls and emails from people who were occupied with other things and did not take the time to call or visit someone who was ill, only to have them die before they got the chance to see or talk to them. Almost always, the situation is similar to yours, and leaves them with horrible feelings and questions like yours: "How do I accept the things I did?"

We'd like to gently correct the idea that you "did" anything wrong or bad. Based on your note, we believe you were trying to get yourself and your son settled in after your move back home. We know that moving is exhausting, both physically and emotionally. We also believe that if you had known just how close your grandma was to the end of her life, you would have dropped everything and run to see her.

In reference to your comment, "I was trying to be strong for my dad and my son"—you can be strong or you can be human—pick one!

From our hearts to yours,
Russell and John

The Good, The Bad, and Sometimes, The Ugly

Anonymous from NM writes:
I lost my brother and feel guilty for not having talked to him for two
months prior to his death. We used to share secrets and always could
count on each other, but now that he's gone I can't get over the grief and
guilt I feel. After an argument, I erased his calls before listening to them
and wish I could take it back.

Dear Anon,
When someone important to us dies, we're often left with
many things we wish had been *different, better, or more.* Sometimes the situation is such that the last interaction we had with
them was a fight or an argument, which leaves us with an additional emotional burden beyond the normal impact of grief
and the things that are never going to happen because the other
person died.

Let us address the word "guilt" as it appears in your note.
Guilt implies intent to harm and, although you may have reacted
to the messages on your answering machine out of some anger
over the argument, our guess is that you didn't do that with an
intent to harm him, and we assume that you certainly didn't
know he was going to die before you got your disagreements
sorted out.

We realize that your awareness doesn't repair the situation,
but the actions of grief recovery do give you a way to address
the undelivered emotions you're carrying with you that you say
you can't "get over."

Relationships have many components—good, bad, and
sometimes ugly. When the last interaction we had wasn't good,
we often carry that last bad interaction forward, and sometimes
lose sight of all the other elements of the relationship.

When you take the actions outlined in *The Grief Recovery*
Handbook you'll learn how to become emotionally complete

with the things that did and didn't happen with your brother so you can remember the whole relationship and not just the ending.

From our hearts to yours,
Russell and John

Sometimes We Have to Break Our Promises

Bertha from MD writes:
Nine months ago my beloved mother died suddenly while in the hospital from an unrelated illness. I was with her almost day and night. Earlier on the day she died, I'd gone home to get some things and, while there, the hospital called and told me that something suddenly happened and my mother had died.

I rushed back to the hospital to find my mother propped up as if for a viewing. I learned from the nurse that she had bled to death but wasn't told why. Since I couldn't get an answer, I had an autopsy done, though my mother hadn't wanted that done under any circumstances.

She died from a condition that my mother and I knew nothing about, something that the doctors could or should have been able to spot and possibly treat. My question is, how do I deal with this emotional trauma? This gaping hole is killing me. I can't help but feel the guilt over the loss, the autopsy, and the guilt over what I might have been able to do.

We were best friends and very close. I was her caregiver and I did not see that ambush coming my way. She was my mom and she trusted me. I feel like I let her down.

Dear Bertha,
Thanks for your note and request for guidance. There are many elements in your note, but we're going to focus on one, the sentence in which you used the word guilt twice: "I can't help but feel the guilt over the loss, the autopsy, and the guilt over what I might have been able to do."

Guilt implies intent to harm. We don't believe you ever had any intent to harm your mother or to overlook anything that might have related to her health. We also believe that you would have done anything and everything that could be done to help her recover and to make sure she wasn't in pain.

With that said, we recommend that you put the word "guilt" back in the dictionary because every time you use it or believe it, you take yourself away from what is devastating you.

More accurately, you might say, "I am devastated by the fact that it seems that the doctors and other professionals at the hospital were unable to see what was actually going on with my mother before it was too late. I'm angry at them for what looks to be a lack of concern and attention to her that caused them to miss seeing what could have saved her life."

We realize that's a rather long and almost academic sounding sentence, but we think it represents something truthful for you. We'd rather you said and felt that so you can shift to the more important task for you, which is focusing on what your mother's death left emotionally unfinished for you. Otherwise you will spend all of your time and energy only on the end of her life, and on the doctors and the hospital, instead of on your lifelong relationship with your mother.

As to the very real issue about the autopsy: Our hearts go out to you on that one. Sometimes we wind up in positions where we feel obliged to break our promises. We believe your need to know what happened was powerful, even though you'd promised you wouldn't. We can't speak for your mother, but we'd guess that she'd truly understand. As you read and take the actions in *The Grief Recovery Handbook,* you'll be able to make the apology about the broken promise, even though it will have to be indirect.

From our hearts to yours,
Russell and John

Walking Through Life Without Your Mate

Ellen from MI writes:
The love of my life died last year unexpectedly. We loved each other very much. Since his death I've read all of his love letters and text messages thousands of times—all of them always saying he could never live without me. I feel very guilty living (if you can call it living) without him. Any advice will be greatly appreciated.

Dear Ellen,
Let us start by saying that this is still very raw for you, just two and a half months of trying to walk through the emotional quicksand of life without your mate. Even though we know time doesn't heal emotional wounds, we do recognize that adapting to the massive changes caused by the death of someone so important to us must be accommodated within time.

Next, let's address the idea of guilt. Guilt implies intent to harm and we have absolutely no sense from reading your note that you ever did anything with intent to harm him.

Rather than guilty, we'd guess that you feel sad, lonely, confused, lost, overwhelmed, and many other feelings in that realm. The problem when you use the wrong word to define your feelings is that it distracts you from your grief and moves you away from the possibility of adapting to this new, disastrous, and unwanted change in your life.

The real key is to begin taking grief recovery actions even while you're learning how to exist—and eventually to do more than just survive—without him here. As you take the actions, you'll begin to find positive shifts in how you feel. You'll be able to retain all the fond and loving memories and, although you naturally will be sad and miss him from time to time, the pain will diminish.

From our hearts to yours,
Russell and John

Left with Unfinished Emotional Business

Gerald from KS writes:

About 25 years ago, my mother and I had a bad argument. Her last words to me were "Get out of my life and stay out! Don't ever contact me again!" I can't tell you how much it hurt to have my own mother say those words to me.

A couple of years ago, on her birthday, I decided to surprise her by sending her a HAPPY BIRTHDAY email. She was surprised all right, but not in the way I had hoped for. I had thought that maybe we could reconcile our differences, and reconnect. Unfortunately, she was against the idea. The more I tried to reason with her, the worse it got. Just the opposite of what I was looking for.

Finally, in her last email, she closed with what seemed very cold to me. "I wish you a long and happy life. Now leave me alone." And, she claims she was bashed all those years. I did not respond and let it go. I see no point in trying a 3rd time. I know she's a heavy smoker, and probably won't live much longer. My question is, when she dies, should I expect to feel any harsh, resentful or guilty feelings, even though I made attempts to clear the negative feelings?

Dear Gerald,

We have to agree with your comment, "I see no point in trying a 3rd time." What would be the point of bashing your head against the same brick wall over and over?

The bigger issue of course is where you ask what you might expect to feel if and when she dies before you. Your point is well taken, that you've made an honest attempt to reconnect, clear the air, and maybe get a fresh start. In fact you made more than one attempt. So from at least that limited perspective, if she should die before you do, you won't be as affected as you might be had you never attempted to reconcile.

That said, we couldn't predict how you might feel any more than you can. If we could, we'd all be at the racetrack because we'd know in advance which horse was going to win. However, given what we know about you and your relationship with/to your mother, we believe that, regardless of your attempts to reconcile, when she dies you will still be left with a lot of unfinished emotional business. The events of twenty-five years ago and everything before and after that are still part of your relationship with her, including your attempts at repair.

We'd suggest you take grief recovery actions now so you can start to feel much more "complete" with what has and hasn't happened over your lifetime with your mother. While it won't preclude you having more feelings, when she dies, you'll be better equipped to deal with those feelings when they happen.

From our hearts to yours,
Russell and John

Hamster on a Wheel

Anonymous from TX writes:

My father died four years ago. It seems like my life is consumed with his death still. Everyday I cry for him, talk to him, and sometimes even act like he didn't die. I know he's never coming back, but I don't want to believe it. He died of lung cancer, and everyday I wonder why. Why him? I get mad at him for dying. I know it's not his fault, but I need someone to blame. And God is out of the picture. Is it normal to still be feeling this horrible?

Dear Anon,

Yes, missing someone you love, talking to someone you love, and crying over their absence are all normal to a large degree, even four years after the death. But if the missing of your father and crying are so constant as to disrupt your ability to function in your life, then it's clear that you need to take actions—which we'll talk about later in this note.

Of course your emotionally poignant question, "Why him?" can't really be answered. We think it represents your broken heart talking. We also believe that your anger and need to blame someone or something are results of your broken heart. As you've probably noticed, you can ask that question a million times and you can still be angry over and over and over, and the question and the feelings don't go away.

Sometimes we notice that grieving people are like hamsters on a wheel, going round and round, and they don't know how to get off the wheel. The more you get caught in the questions, the lament, and the feelings of anger, the more you develop a relationship to or identity with your pain. When your relationship to your pain is that strong, you naturally don't want to give it up. The pain you feel masquerades as love for the person who died, but it isn't really love, it's just pain.

Unfortunately, even if you accept and trust that what we've just said is probably true for you, that knowledge doesn't fix you. That is just awareness or discovery. Discovery without recovery or completion has limited value.

In order to have real changes in how you feel and how you live your life, you're going to have to learn to take the valuable actions of grief recovery. As you do, you'll find the pain, anger, and tears diminishing. You'll find you no longer have a need to ask those questions that can't be answered. And you'll retain all the fond memories you have about the relationship with your father.

From our hearts to yours,
Russell and John

The Nursing Home Facility Mistreated My Mom

Eloise from CT writes:
My mom was 92 years old when she died. She'd lived a long life. I can deal with that and being a good Catholic person, I know she is in Heaven. But what I can't deal with is the way the nursing home facility treated her. I feel awful that I let them get by with what they did to her. They were very mean to her.

Dear Eloise,
Sadly, over the years, we've had many people contact us whose grief was distracted by things that did and didn't happen to their family members in nursing homes. When we say distracted, we mean that your primary focus should be on your relationship with your mom and not on the nursing home.

When you focus on them, you lose sight of your mom. Even though your mom lived a long life and you know she's in Heaven, you probably still feel sad and miss her now that she's gone. You may inadvertently be using the nursing home issues to shield yourself from your feelings about her death.

While it may seem simplistic and difficult to do, you will need to "forgive" the nursing home and the individuals that you believe were mean to your mom so you can get back to focusing on her, not them. It's not fair to your relationship with your mom for you to be using up any emotional energy on them.

In the meantime, if you want to learn more about forgiveness the way we teach it, get a copy of *The Grief Recovery Handbook* and see pages 138, 139, and 140. It will give you a clear idea of how to forgive and what it really means for you.

If you have reason to file a complaint with whichever authority oversees the nursing home, then you are free to do that. We're not saying that forgiveness means you can't make a complaint if it's warranted.

From our hearts to yours,
Russell and John

CHAPTER

FOURTEEN

DEATH, DIVORCE, AND DIFFICULT RELATIONSHIPS: Q&A

On Being "Ruled from the Grave"

Cayla from NY writes:

My mother died suddenly in 2007. We were never close as I grew up because she was abusive and addicted to prescription pain medication. I still feel very angry with her sometimes because of the way our relationship was left when she died. Is it normal to feel angry towards someone who is dead?

Dear Cayla,

The answer is YES! It's very normal to feel anger towards someone who has died. If the relationship was not repaired before she died, her death leaves it in the exact negative condition it was when she was still alive.

You've probably heard the old expression about being "ruled from the grave." This situation is the perfect example of why that expression is so accurate but, as is painfully obvious, you cannot get your mother back alive and talk directly with her in an attempt to repair the damage caused by what she did and didn't do during your childhood.

The good news is that there are things you can do to become emotionally complete with your mother even though she is no longer alive and, in doing that, have some freedom from your past. As you read *The Grief Recovery Handbook* and take grief recovery actions, you'll find your anger diminishing and you'll discover a newfound ability to live more effectively in real time and not in the past.

From our hearts to yours,
Russell and John

When the Last Interaction Was Negative

Anonymous from NV writes:
My sister-in-law died recently. We had a falling out about a year ago.
I apologized to her, but she would never accept my apology, nor see me
again. I'm very saddened by her death. How do I get over this type of
loss when there was no way to reach her before she died?

Dear Anon,
Unfortunately, your story is all too common, where the last interaction between people before one dies was negative. Even in good relationships where the last communications were sweet and loving, the griever is often left with things they wish had happened *differently, better, or more*, and with unrealized *hopes, dreams, and expectations* for the future. This means the unfinished or undelivered communication will have to be dealt with indirectly. For you the issue is NOT just that the last interactions were bad, but that they were *unfinished or incomplete.*

For example, when my mom died suddenly nineteen years ago, I realized I'd never thanked her for not giving up on me as I tried to find my way in life. Since she had died, I couldn't tell her how much I appreciated that directly. So I had to do it indirectly. I tell you that so you can remove the focus from the fact that you cannot get squared away with your sister-in-law, face to face. And I tell it to you so you'll realize it's not just because it was a bad thing or a problem between you at the end, but that it's something you have to deal with on your own now.

Also, I'd guess that there were many more elements to your relationship with her, probably including some good things. You'll need to look at the whole relationship, not just the ending. What I had to communicate to my mother was positive, but I had to communicate my appreciation to her indirectly.

As you read through *The Grief Recovery Handbook* and work your way through the actions it outlines, you'll learn how to get complete with everything that was left unfinished for you with your sister-in-law.

From our hearts to yours,
Russell and John

Confused and Overwhelmed by the Death of a Former Spouse

Anonymous from GA writes:

I just discovered my ex-husband has died. Although he was my ex, I still feel as if a huge part of my life has died with him. No one bothered to tell me, or his child, that he was even ill. I can't stop thinking about him and wishing I could have at least spoken a few last words to him. I hide my grief from my husband. He has no idea how I feel and would not understand, as he's a very jealous man. I'm confused and don't know how to cope with this. When I'm on my own I watch his tribute video and cry with regret. This can't be healthy but I feel so hopeless I don't know what else to do.

Dear Anon,

We're sad to hear about what happened and that you weren't told your ex-husband was ill, and that you were robbed of the opportunity to communicate with him. But we're very glad you've written to us because a great many people are affected by the deaths of their former spouses and are often confused by the tremendous depth of feeling caused by that event. We hope our response helps you and many others.

In *The Grief Recovery Handbook*, we specifically mention "death of a former spouse" as a potential major loss since, by definition, the divorce indicates that the relationship was incomplete. By that we mean, we get married with the hope of going all the way to that happy sunset together. Divorce means that we didn't get to make that dream come true, and along with that comes all the fighting and bitterness that led to divorce.

Since most people don't know how to complete what the divorce left emotionally unfinished for them, they somehow try to get through the worst of the pain of the divorce. Eventually, the pain subsides for most people, and even though that doesn't mean they are "complete" with their ex, they may feel ready to date and remarry.

One of the causes of confusion in the aftermath of divorce or any romantic ending is there's often a feeling of relief that the fighting and other problems are over. That sense of relief creates the illusion of completion with our ex-mates, when it's really relief about the end of the problems. But the original dreams are broken, usually along with a breach of trust and a fear of getting hurt again. So when we start looking for a new love, we may be dragging the emotional baggage from the prior marriage with us.

That's not to say that the new couple can't fall in love and create a wonderful life. Many do. But many of those folks are the ones who are shocked when they discover how much emotion they have when they find out their former spouse has died.

There are two major reasons (and sometimes three) for the emotional impact of the death of the former spouse. First, no matter how painful and awkward the ending was, at one time you loved that person and pledged to love them until the end, even though the end came sooner than you'd hoped. Second, as we indicated above, divorce is a statement of incompleteness and, although the marriage may have ended, the feelings may not have—thus the emotional baggage. The third possible reason is the existence of any children you may have had with your ex, who serve as a constant reminder that the marriage did not make it to that sunset.

With all that in mind, we recommend that you take the actions in *The Grief Recovery Handbook* to help you become emotionally complete with your former spouse who died. As you do this, things should automatically improve with your current husband. He is obviously not the person with whom you ought to share your thoughts and feelings about your ex. You probably want to find a trusted friend who you can talk with as you do the work about your ex. Our other book, *Moving On*, focuses entirely on dealing with divorce and other romantic endings.

From our hearts to yours,
Russell and John

Discovery Does Not Equal Recovery

Vivica from TX writes:

I was divorced five years ago and I was the spouse who filed. I'm feeling increasing despair and sadness as time passes. I'm blaming myself for leaving when I loved my ex-husband. I had unknown past baggage from childhood abuse that I now know affected my ability to be in a marriage with my husband. Now that I know all this, I feel I cannot make peace with the decision to leave. I didn't free myself from problems but instead I found out the source. My life is so much worse since the divorce. Do you have any advice for someone grieving a divorce they initiated and regret? Thanks.

Dear Vivica,

In grief, as in everything else, the old expression about hindsight being 20/20 is still accurate. The problem with your newfound awareness of unresolved grief—as in the baggage from earlier in your life sabotaging your marriage—is that discovery does not equal recovery; and discovery usually doesn't bring our former partners back to us. Most of the time there's been too much damage for the couple to be repaired.

Also, the issue of who initiated the divorce, while it seems important to you, is not the key element. Blaming yourself for leaving is not helping you recover; in fact, it's making it worse. You just keep confirming your pain by stating that you caused it.

Even though the divorce seems to be the burning issue for you, we'll suggest that you first go back and become emotionally complete in your earlier relationships with the people who abused you and/or the people who didn't notice you were being abused or come to your aid, or who possibly didn't believe you.

Until you get complete with those people from your past and the "loss of trust" involved with what happened to you, you won't be able to really get emotionally complete with your ex-husband, nor with yourself for that matter.

Important note: Completion is an indirect action. It's not something you do with the other person/people.

Use the actions in *The Grief Recovery Handbook* to help you go back and deal with the relationships from your distant past. Then, when you've done that, you might consider using *Moving On* to help you deal with the end of your marriage. As you do the work the books ask of you, you'll finally be able to make peace with everything that has happened and then you will be able to restart your life.

From our hearts to yours,
Russell and John

Follow-up Question:
Thank you so much. I am hoping to be able to attend the weekend Grief Recovery Method® Personal Workshop in February, but until then I plan to pick up the book. I also called a local therapist after talking with one of your people today. I've become desperate but honestly, just knowing there's something I can do to facilitate this grief and get better, I feel better already. I had been feeling like this was a downward slide to suicide. Thanks, I'm glad there's help out there for this.

Oh, and after reading your website, I listed all the losses and major changes I've experienced since birth and there are two pages worth. Lots of pain. Seeing it all down in a list was sort of helpful in a way. I have a lot of work to do, including grief about my childhood abuse, my parents' deaths and lack of relationships with them, and my sister's suicide. I know I will heal but it's hard.

Also, while going through this, wouldn't you say it is too soon to try? I know someone who is very nice. He's a good friend of a couple of friends of mine. His wife died two years ago and [he] wants to get to know me. I wonder if it's kind of early. I want to let him know I am not rejecting him, but I am still grieving my marriage and want to wait a little while before dating.

Dear Vivica,

We're incredibly touched by your note, and the obvious hope you have about getting complete with your past so you can create a wonderful future.

We never give advice, but we'd agree with you that it might be best for you to get this work done before you start dating. At this point, you probably realize that the baggage you drag into a new relationship is almost guaranteed to sabotage it.

The good news is that this work doesn't take a very long time. It's about correct actions within time, not just about time.

Something personal from us: Your original, very honest note and your incredibly heartwarming second note in response to our guidance are why we have been doing this for so many years. It makes it all worthwhile. Thank you.

From our hearts to yours,
Russell and John

Families and Legal Mayhem

David from CO writes:
My mother, who died earlier this year, was an extremely private person and wished to keep her financial information from the extended family. She established a trust ten years ago. Due to difficulties with changes in the law, I'm now finding cockroaches creeping from the woodwork, so to speak, and I'm having added stress dealing not only with her death, but also with these people. I feel violated and am experiencing physical symptoms. Please help.

Dear David,
Sadly, your lament is all too common. The stories we hear about what families sometimes do to each other give new meaning to the definition of "enemies." And the legal and government issues we hear about only compound the grief people feel by distracting them from the feelings they are having about the person who died.

There's no simple answer to this kind of situation, and of course, we can't and don't give legal advice. We do suggest that you first do as much as you can to deal with the emotions you have in relationship with your mom who died. The best thing to do is to get started right away with grief recovery actions so that you can complete what was left emotionally unfinished in your relationship with her. As you do that, you'll have more emotional freedom to deal with the troubling ancillary mayhem, and the feelings of violation from the others. We hope this helps.

From our hearts to yours,
Russell and John

The "Warm and Fuzzies" That Never Happened

Penny from AK writes:

My mother died recently at the age of 90, and the Christmas holidays were extremely difficult. Even though my mother lived a long life, we didn't get along too well during my younger days and there was much resentment. Now I feel guilty but devastated that I still bear hard feelings, yet I'm so sad that my mother is gone and we never became loving mother and daughter. How can I overcome the sadness and the guilt?

Dear Penny,

Without diminishing the uniqueness of your relationship with your mother and your very personal feelings, the situation you've described is all too common. Hopefully, our response will not only help you, but will also help untold others who have and continue to struggle with parallel issues. So thank you for bringing up a topic that needs explanation from a grief recovery point of view.

In order to help, we first need to define *grief* and *unresolved grief*. We will use your statements to help do both.

Grief is the conflicting feelings caused by the end of or change in a familiar pattern of behavior. If you're wondering how we might define "conflicting feelings" you don't have to look any further than your own statement, "Now I feel guilty but devastated that I still bear hard feelings, yet I'm so sad that my mother is gone . . ." The conflict is between feeling bad about the hard feelings you still harbor, and your sadness that she is gone.

Unresolved grief is always about undelivered emotional communications that accrue within a relationship over the course of time. Again, a statement in your note defines unresolved grief when you say, ". . . we never became loving mother and daughter." Hearing that, we'd guess the "warm and fuzzies" never happened, and her death ended the hope of that dream ever coming true.

Like you, many people are left with that kind of lament and with the fact that the death has ended the possibility of repair. The naturally occurring feelings of grief—the sadness, the missing of someone (even people with whom we had difficult relationships)—usually subside within time, not as a product of time but as the result of adapting to the new reality of living life without someone important here.

So let's focus on the *unresolved grief,* which is the by-product of what was left emotionally incomplete at the time of the death. Time doesn't do anything to diminish or to finish what was left emotionally incomplete. That's where grief recovery comes in.

It's painful enough to have carried the resentments you had about your mother for all these years, but it would be tragic—for you—to carry them on even after she's gone. At this point, you might be able to see that your resentments—no matter how or by whom they were caused—are now the exclusive creation of your memory. And you are the one carrying them forward, where they can only harm you—and only you.

Unresolved grief drains energy and robs choice. Taking the actions outlined in *The Grief Recovery Handbook* can help you discover and complete everything that was left emotionally unfinished for you in your relationship with your mother who died. As you do that, you'll be able to shed the resentments and other painful emotions you're carrying, and regain energy and choice.

From our hearts to yours,
Russell and John

The Death of the Person Who Harmed You

Patty from FL writes:

My father recently died. We'd been estranged for years. He was a very abusive father, hence the reason I broke off contact. I understand that decision was mine. After his death, I got a call from my mother telling me he'd died and that she'd call me in a few days. The call lasted under a minute, and she never called me again. It's been over a week and I can't reach her. There's been no obituary. I never got any details of a service of any kind. I'm not even sure that I would attend, but I need some kind of closure.

Dear Patty,

We don't use the word "closure" as it implies an end of the relationship—and even the end of memories—which is not accurate or possible. Instead, we prefer to talk about the need for emotional completion, which is exponentially important to anyone whose memory bank is filled with the horrors of abuse.

Even if you knew of a memorial or funeral, and you decided to attend, your presence at such an event would not necessarily give you the "closure" or "completion" you need and want.

A memorial or funeral is effective when it creates an accurate memory picture of the life the person lived. In doing that, it allows each person to recall his or her own relationship with the person who died. But a memorial almost never would include the kind of "truth" that represents what your father did to you, so you'd be liable to leave an event like that with even more bad feelings than you had before.

In essence, your "completion" regarding your father will come as the result of actions you take to discover and complete what's left emotionally unfinished for you, even though you know what happened—that is, you know how badly he treated you. The actions we refer to are presented in detail in *The Grief Recovery Handbook*.

Based on our many years of helping people, we'd guess that your father never acknowledged or apologized for what he did to you. Assuming that to be true, one of the things we know from all the people we've helped is the death of the person who harmed you brings an end to the hope (however unrealistic) that they would someday acknowledge and apologize. Even though you'd broken off contact and moved on in your life, that doesn't mean that you had entirely given up hope that he would someday admit what he'd done and say he was sorry.

From our hearts to yours,
Russell and John

Some Family Members Disassociate Themselves from Others After a Death

Laura from WI writes:
I would just like to know why some family members like to disassociate themselves from other family members after a death?

Dear Laura,
Wow—we don't know if we could answer that apparently simple question even if we had a whole book on the topic. We've heard some of the most horrible stories about the way family members behave towards each other after a death.

Here's a list of probable reasons:

- Some of what happens is an extension of long-term issues between members of the family that may have been hidden.
- Some of what happens relates to money and property and other issues relative to the estate and people's fears of financial insecurity.
- Some of what happens relates to the mass of misinformation many people have about dealing with their own grief and in reacting to the grief of others.
- And very often, a family is loosely held together by their co-relationships to the head of the family—mom, dad, grandma, etc. When that individual dies, the glue that kept the family together loses its hold and, like a house of cards, everything comes tumbling down.

We'd guess that your situation reflects some or all of the above.
While we may have given you some general guidelines in response to your question, there's another question that relates to this secondary loss that follows the death: How do you deal

with the emotions you feel when you are affected by the disassociation, or the splitting up, of the family?

As with all losses, grief recovery actions will help you become emotionally complete with the death of the person who was important to you and will help you deal with the change in or end of relationships with other family members.

From our hearts to yours,
Russell and John

Losses of Safety and Trust—
The Painful By-products of Spousal Abuse

Anonymous from AZ writes:

Is it "normal" for an adult "child" to feel really sad and still grieve 12 years later for an extremely supportive and loving parent who has died? I feel like a little kid in so many ways, looking for that support, missing it. I continue with my life but at times feel as though it happened more recently. I'm also having flashbacks about an abusive marriage, though my kids are all grown. I think this is due to my taking care of my grandchild. What do you think?

Dear Anon,

The range of "normal" feelings relative to grief is quite large. So we can say that to feel sad and miss someone many years later can be normal, but the time element is not the issue. The real question is "what actions have you taken to help you complete what the death of your parent left emotionally unfinished for you?"

Time can't heal emotional wounds and can't complete what was left unfinished. It is the actions *you* take that can help you move from being stuck in grief towards a sense of recovery or completion.

As to your flashbacks about your abusive marriage: You're probably correct that in taking care of your grandkids, you are automatically reminded of your own kids and therefore of your marriage. Again the issue is not of how much time has gone by since the abuse within the marriage, but of what actions you've taken (or not taken) to help you become emotionally complete with the losses of safety, trust, and control that are the painful by-products of spousal abuse.

Since grief is not only about death but about emotions resulting from other losses as well, our hope is that, by taking grief recovery actions, you'll be able to address some of these issues, whether your former spouse is still living or not.

From our hearts to yours,
Russell and John

Alcohol Can Leave a Trail of Destruction in Its Wake!

Anonymous from TX writes:

My husband of twenty-two years died suddenly, after having a wonderful day with his boys, grandchildren, our very close friend, and me. He died alone, at home, and was not found for hours afterwards. He'd been through years of alcohol-related hell, and had just come out of treatment. He was on his way back to his real self. Now he's gone and all that anyone seems to remember about him are the last few years. Why do I have to keep reminding everyone who he really was? I miss him so much. Others are destroying his memory and I see how it hurts our children who are young adults. I'm so torn about how to respond.

Dear Anon,

Sadly, we've heard this kind of problem many times before. Alcoholism, as you know, leaves a trail of destruction in its wake. While you knew the real man underneath the alcohol—and the bad behavior it can sometimes cause—the others may not have known him as well. Some of them may have been hurt by things he did to them. For whatever reasons, they may be unwilling to forgive him.

This may sound a little harsh, but perhaps you have to let them come to whatever conclusions they choose while you focus on dealing with your emotions about his death. The more you do that, the more you'll be able to help your children know what you perceive to be the "real truth" about who their dad was. Eleanor Roosevelt once said, "No one can make you feel inferior without your consent." We would paraphrase that for you to say, "No one can tamper with your memory about your husband without your permission."

From our hearts to yours,
Russell and John

Rather Than Reconcile, Become as Emotionally Complete as Possible

Elizabeth from PA writes:
How does one reconcile an accidental overdose of a twenty-five-year-old child?

Dear Elizabeth,
As short as your note is, it prompts many other questions. If you're referring to an overdose of illegal drugs and it was your child who died, then there's a clear implication that he or she may have been involved in a disease of addiction / dependency of some proportion.

We don't say that to judge but to suggest that if that's true, your relationship with your child who died was more than about how he or she died, it was also about your entire relationship, which would have included all the degrees of difficulties inherent in dealing with someone who struggled with a disease stemming from substance abuse.

The key is not HOW he or she died—intentional or accidental—but THAT he or she died. We will guess that your heart is 100 percent broken and would be in either case.

Also, we want to address the issue of trying to "reconcile" the event. The dictionary defines reconcile as: *to cause [a person] to accept or be resigned to something not desired.* We don't think you ever can really reconcile what happened, though life forces you to resign yourself to the reality of it.

Rather than reconcile, we encourage you to take actions to become as emotionally complete as you can with the relationship you had with your child before the death; to become as emotionally complete as you can with how the death happened; and to become as emotionally complete as you can with all the now-broken *hopes, dreams, and expectations* you had for your child's future and your presence in that future.

As you take grief recovery actions, you'll begin to feel emotionally complete and with that will come a reduction in the pain you've probably been feeling. That doesn't mean you will never be sad or miss your child, but there will be a shift that allows you to move forward in your life, even though the death has dramatically affected you.

From our hearts to yours,
Russell and John

CHILDREN: Q&A

Putting Together a Puzzle with Very Few Pieces

Melissa from AR writes:
Does the grief of losing a parent and family you never met ever go away? My father was killed in Vietnam while my mother was pregnant. I never met the family. Now, as I look, I'm finding they all died at young ages. I cry often. I don't know my own family. No pictures, no memories, no family left to find, maybe cousins but . . .

Dear Melissa,
The questions about whether any grief ever goes away is one we get very often—whether it relates to someone you knew or to someone who you never even met.

Your situation is parallel in many ways to that of people who were adopted who spend much of their lives trying to put together a puzzle with very few pieces. As to whether or not the grief ever goes away, it's most helpful to suggest that until or unless you take some actions to "discover and complete" what was left emotionally unfinished for you by the absence of your dad in your life—even if you had a stepfather—then you're liable to loop the grief feelings over and over.

With that in mind, please get a copy of *The Grief Recovery Handbook*, available in most libraries and bookstores. You'll notice that it is the *Twentieth Anniversary Expanded Edition*, and one of the main reasons we added some new material was so we could address the issues that are affecting you.

If you open the book to page 174, you'll find the heading, "Death or Absence of a Parent from an Early Age." Read that section on pages 174 and 175. Then go back to the beginning and start reading the book and taking the actions it suggests. We know it will help you.

From our hearts to yours,
Russell and John

A Recurring Dream . . . After 58 Years

Thomas from UT writes:

My father died when I was five years old. I am now fifty-eight. I've had a recurring dream all of my life in which I'm running towards my dad as he calls to me, but when I'm almost to him the ground gives way, I begin to free-fall, and then awaken. When I awake I feel like crying and it's usually very hard for me to get back to sleep. I have this dream several times per year and usually when I am stressed about something. Is this unusual? Is it unresolved grief? I find it hard to talk about this to anyone I know.

Dear Thomas,

No, it is not unusual to have recurring dreams over a lifetime. Many people do. Since your dad died when you were so young, it makes sense that you would have a powerful relationship to the images in the dream, as they obviously represent a connection to him.

It's interesting and logical that the dream tends to surface when you're feeling stressed. Since the dream itself could be called stressful, it kind of shows how the feelings that surface in our dreams tend to mimic what's happening in our waking life.

Also, we'd assume that since you were so young when he died, you have relatively few conscious memories and images of him, so again it makes sense to have one recur, even in dream form. Whether or not it represents unresolved grief is a question we can't answer definitively. That said, we'd guess there's a very high probability that you have more than a little unresolved grief about the relationship with your father whom you barely knew, and who was not there for most of your life.

After taking grief recovery actions, the dream may disappear or modify as you remember and complete other aspects of your relationship with your father. We notice that you said you find it hard to talk about this with anyone, so we want to say "Thank you" for trusting us with this—we know it has a lot of emotional meaning for you.

From our hearts to yours,
Russell and John

Missing People We Never Really Knew

Jamie from MI writes:
I lost my dad when I was two. I'm 18 now. Is it normal not to be over the fact that he's gone?

Dear Jamie,
Let's start with the idea that your life was very much affected by the death of your dad. Since you were so young when he died, we'd guess you have very few conscious memories about him. We'd also guess that as a little girl you were very much affected by your mom's grief and how she dealt with her reaction to your father's death.

Now, let's talk about the fact that it's normal to miss people who are important to us, even if they're still alive and perhaps live far away. It's also very normal to miss your dad all these years later, even though, as we said, you might not have many real memories of him.

As to "being over" the fact that he's gone, in our book, *The Grief Recovery Handbook,* we talk about the idea that "getting over" someone who was important to us implies forgetting them. Even though you probably don't have a lot of memories about your dad, the fact is you're not going to forget the idea of him and you're not going to stop having feelings about him.

Getting to your current age, it makes sense that you might have very strong feelings about the absence of your dad in your life—not only now, but over all of the past sixteen years. And yes, that's all very normal.

As always, we suggest that instead of trying to "get over" your dad, you take grief recovery actions to help you discover and complete everything that was left emotionally incomplete for you by his death.

From our hearts to yours,
Russell and John

My Daughter Wants to Take the Plane to Heaven to See Her Grandpa

Allie from WA writes:
My dad died last year and my three-year-old daughter misses him very much. I know that's okay, but more than once she's asked me if she can take the plane to go to heaven to see him. I'm getting concerned. Can you help me?

Dear Allie,

Young minds are very impressionable and take the things they hear from the adults around them very literally. Whether you see heaven as an actual place or think of it more in a metaphorical sense, we can assure you that your little one thinks of it as a real place.

She's in that age bracket where it would be difficult to explain the difference to her. That's why we devote a chapter in *When Children Grieve* (pages 230–234) to the topic of metaphors and euphemisms, and how they can cause confusion for young children. The classic example of a metaphor confusing young children is when adults refer to death as "sleep." Many children have been terrified to go to sleep after having viewed grandpa in a casket and being told he was sleeping.

In that chapter in our book, we wrote about the specific issue you're concerned about: "Most people allude to heaven being up above. Small children take that very literally, also. We have been told many times of children looking out of airplane windows, trying to find Grandpa." Please take the time to read the whole chapter. It will help you explain to her what heaven means to you, without modifying any religious or spiritual beliefs you may have.

From our hearts to yours,
Russell and John

"Monkey See, Monkey Do"

Janice from IL writes:

My ex-husband committed suicide in August. We have a four-year-old daughter together. We'd remained friends for her sake and ours as well. He was going through a hard time with a recent loss of his job and divorce from his second wife. He'd call me and we'd talk. He had a "breakdown" and received treatment. Unfortunately, between the therapy and medication it wasn't enough. I deal with this guilt that if he had called me that night I could have helped him. I had a feeling a couple of days prior that he may do this because of events that had happened years ago. But after we talked, I thought he was all right. The night it happened my heart broke from the years of friendship we had, the child we had together who will miss her father, and for his family.

How do I know that although my daughter appears happy and well adjusted this won't negatively impact her in the future? What impact will this have on her? We talk about him often and she asks to visit the grave. She doesn't appear scared in any way and will tell people about her dad and how he is in Heaven. Like any mother feels, she is the center of my world, and I love her beyond words. I want to do the best for her.

Dear Janice,

We're not surprised at the amount of emotion you have about his death. After all, divorce is about relationships that don't make it all the way to that happy sunset when both spouses are in their nineties. That means there's usually a great deal of unresolved or unfinished business, which is what causes the divorce in the first place. When someone we used to be married to dies, we often experience a re-remembering of the entire relationship, the good, the bad, and the sometimes ugly. For you, the divorce, and now his death are compounded by the fact that he was your daughter's father and she will always be a reminder to you about him.

About your daughter and her future: We can't predict what will happen as she gets a little older and starts to realize exactly what it all means. At this point, she probably doesn't understand the permanence of death, which is why she may not seem scared, and why she can easily say the things she does about him being in heaven.

Your concern for her well-being is exactly as it should be. Our book, *When Children Grieve*, will help you guide her as her life unfolds, especially in relation to the absence of her father. It will also help guide you in taking care of your own grief, since she will be learning from you and copying what you do. Fittingly, the first chapter in the book is, "Monkey See, Monkey Do."

From our hearts to yours,
Russell and John

An Eleven-Year-Old's Upset Reactions to Questions about Death

Anonymous from AL writes:
My eleven-year-old daughter's father died two years ago, and her Granny died recently. She seems to get angry when people speak about her father and upset when they ask how she is doing. Is this a normal reaction?

Dear Anon,

It may surprise you to learn just how normal your daughter's reaction is—especially when she's asked how she's doing. If people weren't generally so polite in response to the question, "How are you doing," many would say, angrily, "How do you think I'm doing? My father died, or my granny just died, or my husband, or my child, etc."

To explain it a little more, if we had to guess, your daughter has probably had the experience of having her feelings rebuffed when she told the truth. For example, if people asked her how she was doing and she told them, "I'm hurting" or "I'm having a hard time," they may have said to her, "Well, don't feel bad, Granny's in a better place." It doesn't take many incidences of having your honest feelings slapped down to learn to dislike questions about how you feel.

Also, we don't think it's a good idea to ask people how they feel or how they're doing, because it somehow becomes interrogative. What we suggest is, "I heard that your daddy died, and I can't imagine what this has been like for you." That's really a statement that is turned into a question by raising your voice at the end. There's something about the word "imagine" that makes it soft and noninvasive, and also tells the griever that you will not judge them for their answer. With that, it's important that when someone does tell you how they feel or how they're really doing, you don't judge them for feeling that way.

We'd also guess that your daughter is emotionally incomplete with her father, not because of anything she's done or not done but because his death automatically created unfinished business for her. We recommend that you go to a bookstore or library and get a copy of *When Children Grieve*. Reading it will help you talk with her and possibly guide her to some grief recovery actions that will help her as it relates to her father and to her granny.

From our hearts to yours,
Russell and John

Helping Children in Foster Care Deal with Multiple Losses

Caroline from VA writes:

Can you tell me a little more about the issues children specifically face? I work with children who have been taken into foster care and then adopted. So, in my terms there is a "necessary grief" as they have had a loss imposed on them in order to save their lives. I would love your perspective on things I might do especially when so many of the children I work with don't have the level of insight to approach this analytically. Looking forward to your reply with interest.

Dear Caroline,

Without a doubt, children who've been taken into foster care have already experienced at least one if not several major losses. However, depending on their ages, their perception and memory of what has happened may be limited.

The memory experts suggest that the dawn of conscious memory is somewhere between the ages of three and six, usually closer to six. That does not mean that children are not affected by what does and doesn't happen before then, only that their ability to remember the events and attached feelings later may be very limited, if available at all, especially while they are still young. That, in part, is what we think you're referring to when you say they don't have the "level of insight."

This reality makes it even more important that those who care for children in foster care, adoptive, or other situations be as schooled as possible in dealing with the emotions that emerge as those children barge through life. If, at the very least, those children can be given an accurate and helpful foundation for dealing with grief (and they will have other losses to confront as their lives unfold), they will have a better chance at successful and happy lives.

Our book, *When Children Grieve: For Adults to Help Children Deal with Death, Divorce, Pet Loss, Moving, and Other Losses,* addresses many of the issues that you face on a regular basis in working with the children. The book also addresses the varying levels of perception based on the age of the child. After you've read the book, please don't hesitate to contact us and we can discuss this further.

From our hearts to yours,
Russell and John

Explaining Death to Young Children and to a Child with Special Needs

Vera from PA writes:

How can I explain the death of my parent to my child with special needs—autism? She's eight years old, diagnosed as "mild," and presents with ADD on a mild scale. She's able to communicate relatively well. When she describes "grandma's house" she immediately states that she and her aunt live there. As far as her cognitive ability is concerned, she can easily play video games and knows not to touch the stove. She was very close to her grandmother who would care for her whenever I had to work late or had to leave town on business. She could quickly pick her out in a crowded room and freely accepted and gave affection to her.

Dear Vera,

Given her age and the other factors you mention, we'd assume that she certainly has seen dead leaves that fall from trees and she has probably seen dead animals. Nature—in those forms—is generally the best pathway to explain death to all kids, and since her comprehension is good, she should be able to understand.

However, one key issue for young children is they often don't yet understand the "permanence" of death. Your daughter is right on the outer cusp line for that understanding, whereas if she were only three, four, five, or even six, she might have a hard time with that. Explain death as best you can to her using age-appropriate language and concepts and, if need be, with any other consideration that you deem best since you probably know her better than anyone in the world.

After you have set up the idea of death and what it is, you can tell her about Grandma. It may be emotional for you and, if so, let that be—let her see your emotions, but don't let her try to "fix" you. Explain that tears and sadness are normal reactions when someone we love dies. As sad as it may seem, it can be a superb teaching event which will help her with the other loss events that will occur in her lifetime.

It may or may not be emotional for her as she may not immediately comprehend that it means that she will never get to see her grandmother again—at least not here on earth—but don't be preoccupied if she's not emotional. It may take her a while to make sense of it all. The first holiday or birthday that grandmother would normally attend may be when it hits her.

You definitely want to avoid euphemisms because children are so literal. Don't say "Grandma's gone" or "We've lost Grandma." And even if you believe in heaven, don't say "Grandma's gone to heaven." What you'd say is "Grandma died, and we believe that when people die they go to heaven." It's very important to separate that into those two parts. If you don't make that clear, the child will want to go to heaven and see Grandma.

Also, be really clear with your language when talking about yourself as it relates to Grandma's death. Say things like "I'm very sad" and "I miss her very much." That way you teach her how to communicate her own feelings. We strongly suggest you go to the bookstore or library and get a copy of our book, *When Children Grieve: For Adults to Help Children Deal with Death, Divorce, Pet Loss, Moving, and Other Losses*. It has in-depth explanations about some of the things we've touched upon in this note.

From our hearts to yours,
Russell and John

Whether or Not to Take Children to Funerals or Memorials

Harold from IL writes:

My wife died last year in tragic circumstances. My young granddaughter and grandson witnessed the event and made attempts to save her. There was a lot of media coverage of the event and the children are going to be honored for their valor in trying to come to her rescue. I would like them to attend the banquet at which they would be honored, but I'm concerned that it might bring back painful memories for them. Do you think the children should attend?

Dear Harold,

What a powerful and painful story. In our book, *When Children Grieve,* we address the issue of whether or not to take children to funerals or memorials. The short chapter is called *Four Weddings and a Funeral* and it begins on page 234 of the book. Make sure you read that section before deciding if you think it best for either or both of your grandchildren to attend the event, since there will be things said and shown that will be very emotional. That's a not a bad thing, but something that you'd want to prepare them for. Make sure you follow the guidelines in the book about explaining what's going to happen so they can participate in the decision of whether or not to go.

Also, before you have that chat with them, find out if the evening is going to be videotaped. If so, you can tell that to the children, who could choose not to go, knowing that they could watch it at a later date.

We can tell you that many who come to our seminars and trainings carry forward a life-long complaint of NOT having been allowed to attend certain events, thereby robbing them of a chance to say goodbye and other communications.

As to the "painful memories": They are there whether or not the children go to the event. Avoiding talk about the event, about

Grandma, or other reminders isn't necessarily good, and those memories may get buried deeper and erupt later with unforeseen consequences.

After you've had a chance to read the chapter, feel free to call or email us with further questions.

From our hearts to yours,
Russell and John

Are Bedwetting and Grief Related?

Carrie from MD writes:
My ex-husband died at age thirty-five. We have two little girls together. They are six and four years old. My six year old has started wetting her pants at least once a day. What should I do about it? I've been told that it could be a sign of grief but I don't know.

Dear Carrie,
The range of "normal" reactions to the death of someone important to a child is very wide, and what's going on with your daughter is well within that range. To explain what's going on with your older girl, we would say, "In a crisis we go back to old behaviors or old beliefs." We'd guess that your daughter probably had broken the habit of bed- or pants-wetting some time ago, but the untimely death of her father has brought back something old and familiar. (Keep in mind that people who've quit smoking or drinking or overeating will sometimes relapse after the death of someone important to them—again with the idea that they return to something old and familiar).

At her age, she's probably much more aware of what death means than your four-year-old is. The younger one might appear from time to time to be unaffected by her dad's death, but she probably doesn't understand the permanence of death yet.

The first thing we'd suggest is that you not be upset with your daughter—that you not scold her or judge her in any way. We'd guess that she may already be embarrassed by what's happening so she needs as much safety as she can get from you. Give her a little time in which to adapt to the fact that with her daddy's death, her world is upside down. If the pants wetting doesn't subside in a few weeks and you are concerned, then call your pediatrician.

Next, we'd suggest you go to the library or bookstore and get a copy of our book, *When Children Grieve*. The subtitle of the book is, *For Adults to Help Children Deal with Death, Divorce, Pet Loss, Moving, and Other Losses*. It's filled with information that will help you guide your children as the three of you deal with this new, painful reality.

From our hearts to yours,
Russell and John

Three Little Girls Ask When Daddy Will Be Home

Jessica from VT writes:
My husband died in July last year. It still feels like yesterday and I'm so heartbroken it's unbelievable. I have three little girls and they're so sad and ask often when will he be home? Lots of people tell me I have to let him rest and not talk about him so much or go visit him at the cemetery. Am I wrong to hold on so strong?

Dear Jessica,
We don't think you're wrong for talking about him or visiting the cemetery. Nor do we think the things you do or don't do affect him being at "rest." Although, what you do affects the degree to which you are able to be present to help and guide your girls.

We certainly understand your need and desire to "hold on to him so strongly" because your heart is so incredibly broken. Grief is hard enough for all of us without having people tell us incorrect things about how we should feel and what we should do.

Your note doesn't give the ages of your girls, which makes it difficult to give you specific guidance. Since their ages dictate their ability to comprehend what has happened, which in turn affects their emotions, we'll direct you to our book, *When Children Grieve*. It explains in more detail than we can give you here things that relate to different age brackets and children's understanding of the permanence of death.

As for you and your grief: If you take grief recovery actions outlined in *The Grief Recovery Handbook* in relation to your own reactions to the death of your husband, you'll find a shift occurring that will help you stay present and also help you communicate openly in ways that will help the girls do the same.

From our hearts to yours,
Russell and John

Helping a Four-Year-Old Know Who His Mother Really Was

Patty from IN writes:
My sister died when I was twenty-five and five months pregnant. She was my life, heart, soul, and blood. She left behind a four-year-old little boy who misses her dearly. She was the only sister I had. How do I cope with losing my heart?

Dear Patty,
One of the most difficult things to do is to find a way to deal with the untimely death of someone of massive importance to us. And with that, to learn to adapt to your new life and move forward in spite of what has happened. As we'd imagine you've already figured out, time doesn't make it any better—in fact for many people it seems worse as time goes by if they haven't taken any actions of recovery.

One of the things we hope will help you is the idea that you must be one of the people who help her son know who his mother really was. While he will have some memories of her later, it will be up to you to really tell him about her. But in order to do that, you will have to become emotionally complete so that you will not be afraid to remember her, talk about her, and share her with him and others.

Grief recovery will guide you through this process and you'll begin to feel your heart coming back.

Also, *When Children Grieve* is a superb book for you and the other adults who will be guiding your nephew as he begins to understand the painful reality of what has happened.

From our hearts to yours,
Russell and John

Going to Church Reminds a Twelve-Year-Old of His Dad's Death

Barbara from GA writes:
How can you help a twelve-year-old boy who finds his only parent (father) dead in his bed on Christmas morning? Living arrangements are fine, but the boy will not go to church, and has not been forced to go.

His aunt is seeking guardianship and he has a grandma—my sister—both of whom he has been close to since birth. They live within minutes of each other, so they're sharing his care. Grandma is probably his closest bond and she sees him daily. She feels too old to have him full-time as she is seventy-one. He's gone to the same church since birth, where his aunt and Grandma go. The father's funeral was in the church, and the boy will not go in the church now. He has talked with the pastor, but no one knows exactly why he won't go in. So far, they have just taken him home when he refuses to go.

Dear Barbara,
What a difficult situation. There's a big tip-off in your note that may contain the underlying truth about the church issue. Even though the lad has talked to the pastor, the actual church building may be a massive stimulus for him since that's where the funeral service was held. The memories of that event may cause him so much emotion about the death of his father that he just can't be in the building, not to mention the terrible imagery he carries forward of finding his dad dead on Christmas morning. In addition to that, although we don't know the circumstances surrounding the fact, he apparently doesn't have a living mother.

Unresolved grief is cumulative and cumulatively negative, and the stimulus of the church itself may bring up all of his past for him. Clearly his life has not been lived in the way most children's lives are—with the death and with a lot of moving and a variety of guardians.

We realize it may not seem logical to you but to us it's very typical, if not almost predictable. There's one more outstanding question for us to ask. The question is whether or not the boy has always been eager to go to church these past many years or if he was going out of obligation to the adults who took him. If he felt forced to go, we aren't surprised that he might rebel now. Either way, we still think that since the funeral was in the church, the highest probability is that he associates his dad's death with that place.

There's another possible factor also. Many people interpret their religious teachings to indicate that God has an absolute and direct power of life and death over each of us. For children, that is often a literal belief rather than a figurative one. It's very possible that the child is angry with God for taking his dad away. And it's not a stretch to say that the church is God's house, so the boy could be angry with that place as well as with God. One last thing, even if the pastor chatted with him, he might have been afraid to admit or show his anger at God—if that is the case.

We don't give direct advice regarding actions anyone might take in this kind of situation, but we'll give you our opinion to consider. We'd suggest that *for now*, you not push the issue of going to church. If you force him to go, you might do more harm than good as well as push him away from God and your family's religion for the rest of his life. We think there's less risk in letting him not attend—without judgment or criticism from any of you who are around him—thereby allowing him to make his own private peace with God, the way he sees and interprets God.

Giving him the freedom and dignity to find his own solution may encourage him to be open and honest with one or more of you. If he feels safe enough that he could talk about his thoughts and feelings without fear of judgment or reprisal, he may open up as to why he doesn't want to go to church, along with a host of other things he may not be talking about.

Over the past twenty-five years we've discovered that if we help people deal effectively with the death that has affected them—and often with it their anger at God or the church because of the nature or circumstances of the death—then later we can help them get close again with God if they so desire.

One key to the grief aspect of this, which is of course immense, is for all of you adults to be open and honest about your feelings about the death of his father. And you each need to talk about your relationships with his dad. By so doing, you will be demonstrating healthy expression of emotion that he can copy.

From our hearts to yours,
Russell and John

IN CLOSING

One of the most common personal questions we get is, "Isn't it depressing, working with grievers and grief every day?"

We understand that people might think that because most folks think only of grief without recovery. They think we just listen to people telling stories of their emotional pain over and over.

Nothing could be further from the truth. While we do hear more than our fair share of heartrending stories, most of what we do, even when we first interact with a griever, is to help them understand that what they're feeling is normal and natural, that they're not crazy.

From that starting point, the interaction is not about them venting their feelings to a stranger—it's about acquiring helpful information that will guide them to discovering and completing everything that was left emotionally unfinished for them with the person who died. As you've read this book, you've seen that last sentence or variations on it many times. And we add it here because it's the essential idea that we are trying to communicate to give people hope that recovery is possible.

Speaking of hope: That's the desired result of the first inter-action we have with someone. So many people who find us seem to have almost given up hope that they can ever feel different or better than they do. We say almost because if they've truly given up, they're not liable to call The Grief Recovery Institute.

If you could listen in on one of the calls we get, you'd hear a fascinating transition within ten or fifteen minutes. Often, when the call first starts, we can hardly hear the caller. And what we do hear sounds lifeless, without energy. But very quickly as we talk and listen, something starts to shift for them. They start to feel heard, and they realize that the things we say are different than the kinds of things other people have been saying to them.

On our end of the phone, we hear the voice come up and energy come into their communication. With that also comes the hope that something different is possible for them. And we have done the first part of our job.

So when people ask if what we do is depressing, our answer is "No, it's uplifting." Nearly every interaction we have with grieving people ends on a high note. For us, the personal reward is beyond words.

We hope that, in addition to gaining some valuable informa-tion, including the fact that you are not the only one having some of the thoughts and feelings you've had in reaction to losses, you will finish this book with your own sense of hope for your future.

From our hearts to yours,
Russell and John

Time Doesn't Heal—Actions Do

I have heard that it takes two years to get over the death of a loved one, five years to get over the death of a parent, and you never get over the death of a child. Is this true?

It is impossible to answer that question without first debunking the phrase "get over." You will never forget your child who died, nor would you forget a parent who died, or a spouse, a sibling, or anyone else with whom you had a meaningful relationship. Another problem is the arbitrary determination of time periods for grief corresponding to your relationship with the person who died.

Those time-based criteria make crippling and illogical comparisons between relationships and your feelings about them. Since no two relationships are ever the same, it is never helpful to compare your reaction to the death of someone important to you with any other loss—someone else's or your own.

Grieving people are confronted with an unbelievable amount of uncontested misinformation. Immediately following a death, grievers are hit with ideas that are not only incorrect but suggest that recovery from the pain caused by death is solely a function of time or, in some situations, that it isn't even possible.

The assumption that time heals emotional wounds is so prevalent that we include it as one of the six myths that most limit grieving people. Imagine that you have gone out to your car and discovered that it has a flat tire. Would you pull up a chair, sit down, and wait for air to get back into your tire? Obviously not. Time is not going to put air into your tire. Only the actions of fixing or changing the flat tire will get the car back on the road.

The same is true of grief. Time can't do any more for your broken heart than it can for a flat tire. It is equally true that only correct actions can help you complete what was left unfinished between you and someone who died so that you can get your life back on the road.

Not the Time for a Debate

Since grievers are reeling under the impact of a death, they usually don't stop to analyze and debate the bad advice they receive. Without accurate and helpful guidance, they simply cling to the myth that time heals because they have nothing to believe in its place. The idea that time can repair an emotional wound is not only false, it is also dangerous because it stops grievers from learning what actions would help them deal with the inevitable discoveries they make of things that were left incomplete in their relationship with the person who died.

Why Does the Myth That Time Will Heal Persist?

Like many misleading ideas, the notion that time heals has a partial basis in reality. Recovery from loss and completion of emotional pain is the result of small and correct action choices taken over time that lead to successful completion of what the death left emotionally unfinished for you.

There is a world of difference between time healing a wound and a wound healing over time as the result of actions.

Let us try to explain how an aspect of truth dictates the falsehood. Death of someone important to us can produce an overwhelming amount of emotional energy. At times the pain is so unbearable that our hearts and brains numb us out when it is too much for us to handle. We call it emotional Novocain, a metaphor that helps people understand what they are experiencing.

Numbness notwithstanding, in time most people adapt to the reality of the loss. As that occurs, some of the pain will diminish naturally. Most people interpret the reduced pain to have been caused by the passage of time, since that's what they were taught to believe. But that's not true. It is the natural survival ability to adjust to the altered circumstances of your life that creates the illusion that time has healed you.

Even though most people find a way to accommodate the new reality of their lives after someone important dies, that does not mean they have completed what was left unfinished. That is why so many people tell us that even years after the death, they feel the pain is getting worse, not better. For them, time is an enemy, not a friend.

The key to dealing with the impact of the death of someone important to you is not to wait for time to do what it cannot do, but to take the actions that will help you complete what the death left unfinished. The actions of grief recovery are spelled out in detail in *The Grief Recovery Handbook*, which is available at most libraries and bookstores.

On Crying—Part One

Almost everyone has some questions and confusion about crying. How much crying is enough? If I start crying, will I be able to stop? Do I have to cry at all? I've cried and cried but I still don't feel better; is there something wrong with me? Are men and women different when it comes to crying? We will address these and other questions in this two-part series on crying. We had intended this to be a single article, but as it unfolded we realized that it needed more than a little space to do it justice. Do not be alarmed if you recognize yourself in some of the scenarios highlighted here.

A common call to The Grief Recovery Institute starts like this: "My mom died several months ago, and I'm very worried about my dad." This statement is made by a young man or woman who is concerned about the well-being of his or her father. In the ensuing conversation, we determine that although the caller believes that Dad is devastated by the death of his spouse, Dad has not cried "yet." We have put the word yet in quotes to illustrate the son or daughter's obvious belief that in order to grieve you must cry. (The fact is that the son or daughter has not seen him cry. That does not mean that Dad has not cried in private, and either has not or will not talk about it.) The well-meaning offspring is concerned because they believe that there is an absolute and direct correlation between grief and crying. When asked if they think that Dad's heart is broken, they always respond that they are sure that it is. We ask them, "Where is it written that you must cry when you are sad?" We do not ask that question to be mean-spirited, but merely to illustrate that the caller may be laboring under a terrible misapprehension that tears must accompany sad feelings.

Let us pose a couple of other questions here, as we do in person or on the telephone. Have you ever known anyone who cries all the time, but never seems to change or grow? Have you ever known anyone who uses crying as a manipulation to get something? There is a high probability that you will answer yes to both questions. Both of those questions are designed to explain the fact that crying, in and of itself, does not necessarily lead to completion of the pain caused by death, divorce, or any other losses. At best, crying acts as a short-term energy relieving action and relieves, temporarily, some of the emotional energy generated by the loss. We know of people who have been crying over the same loss, daily, for years and years. We know that the crying has not helped them complete what is emotionally incomplete in their relationship with their loved one who died, or the person from whom they are divorced.

As our society has evolved, we have seen a quantum shift in the public display of emotion. In today's world, it is not at all unlikely to see a retiring professional athlete, often the paragon of masculinity, weeping openly in a televised press conference. It is hard to imagine that same scenario occurring thirty or forty years ago. If your male parent is seventy years old or older, he is more likely to be affected by different beliefs about the open display of emotions than you are. Even your female parent is liable to be less willing to communicate sad, painful, or negative emotions than you. You must fight the trap of applying your emotional value system to others. It may seem odd, since your parents taught you, that you have different emotional views than they do.

In part two we will address issues of gender and the underlying keys to recovery based on the uniqueness of each individual relationship.

Question: If I start crying, will I be able to stop?

Answer: In our years of helping grieving people, we have never seen anyone who has been unable to stop crying.

On Crying—Part Two

In "On Crying—Part One," we focused on the idea that it can be dangerous and counterproductive to attach our personal ideas and beliefs to how other people express their grief, given the fact that many people will communicate tremendous depth of emotion and never shed a tear while others cry all the time but don't seem to complete the pain nor derive any long term benefit from crying. In part two, we are going to address issues of gender and uniqueness of individuals and relationships as well as exactly what function crying serves and for whom.

We are aware of the research that indicates that tears of sadness differ in chemical makeup from tears of joy. We are also aware that tears perform the valuable function of washing the eyes. From time to time, we have even alluded to the published studies that indicate that women cry, on average, five times more than men. In attempting to discover if there is any physiological basis for that five-to-one ratio, we ran into a stone wall.

Failing to find any valid studies on crying that would support a physical distinction by gender, we did a little of our own research. While anecdotal, we believe that it represents the truth. We called some nurse friends whose life experience is working with infants. Without exception, they indicated to us that the circumstances and frequency with which very young infants cry is NOT dictated by gender. Little baby boys and little baby girls cry equally. There are clear personality differences between individual babies. Some cry more than others, not by gender but rather by individual uniqueness. We did not limit our search to those who worked only with newborns. We got the same responses from experts who work with children up to the age of five. From age five onwards, distinction by gender and the resultant attitudes and beliefs begin to magnify. The logical extension of our informal study led to the inescapable conclusion that socialization, not gender, was the key to later differences of attitude and expression regarding crying.

Although there may be no innate physiological difference between males and females when it comes to crying, we must still ask, what purpose or value, if any, does crying have in recovery from loss? Let us say that crying can represent a physical demonstration of emotional energy attached to a reminder of someone or something that has some significance for you. In fact, during our grief recovery seminars when someone starts crying, we gently urge them to "talk while you cry." The emotions are contained in the words the griever speaks, not in the tears that they cry. What is fascinating to observe is that as the thoughts and feelings are spoken, the tears usually disappear and the depth of feeling communicated seems much more powerful than mere tears. In "On Crying—Part One," we talked with an adult child whose Mom had died. The caller was worried about their dad's reaction to Mom's death, and the fact that Dad had not cried "yet." We asked the caller if they thought that their dad's heart was broken. They said yes. We believed that their response, based on their observations of Dad's body language, tone, and other factors, showed them that he had been immensely affected by the death of his wife. It would be unusual, uncommon, and probably uncomfortable for him to cry and, frankly, it might not have any real benefit for him.

On the other hand, do not be fooled by those who cry frequently. In one of the strangest of all paradoxes, people can actually use crying as a way to stop feeling rather than to experience great depths of emotion. The tears become a distraction from the real pain caused by the loss.

The key to recovery from the incredible pain caused by death, divorce, and all other losses is contained in a simple statement: Each of us is unique and each of our relationships is unique. Therefore, we must discover and complete what is emotionally unfinished for us in all of our relationships. Our personal belief systems about the display of emotions are also unique and individual. We may not even have a conscious awareness of what our own beliefs are. An alert to everyone, young or old: "Don't let anyone else dictate what is emotionally correct for you—not even your children or your parents. Only you get to determine what is correct for you."

If you need some help in discovering or determining what might help you deal with a broken heart caused by a death or a divorce, get thee to a library or a bookstore and get a copy of *The Grief Recovery Handbook*. It contains the kind of information that will lead you to your truth, which in turn will help you complete the actions required to lessen the pain in your heart.

Please do not interpret this article to mean that we are in any way against crying. What we do prompts tears all the time. At the restaurant across the street where we take our friends to lunch, they don't understand why everyone who dines with us seems to cry. And if you visited our office, you would have to giggle when you see the gigantic stack of cases of Kleenex piled in a corner of the room. We are neither for nor against crying. We are for recovery from emotional pain. We are for fond memories that do not turn painful. We are for you having a life of meaning and value even though a loss or losses may have made your life drastically different than what you had hoped or dreamed.

Normal and Natural Reactions to Death

Grief is the wide range of normal and natural reactions to the death of someone important to you. The seven most common reactions are:

- Numbness
- Reduced Ability to Concentrate or Focus
- Crying or NOT Crying
- Lowered State of Energy—Not To Be Confused with Clinical Depression
- Disturbed Sleeping Patterns
- Dreams and Nightmares
- Irregular Eating Patterns
- Roller Coaster of Emotions

If you're reading this, it's likely that someone important to you has died and you'd like some guidance about the feelings and thoughts you're experiencing. Or you may be reading this because you are connected to and concerned about someone who's just experienced a death, and you'd like to have more awareness about what they're going through, and what you can say or do to be helpful to them.

Confusion about What Is Normal in an Unfamiliar Situation

While it's true that grief is the normal and natural reaction to a death, fortunately most of us don't have that experience very often, which makes it unfamiliar. Also, grief is not generally an open topic of conversation in our society and a great deal of the information available to us about grief is not accurate or helpful.

With those ideas as a start point, grieving people are often confused by their reactions to a death. It's helpful to be aware of the range of normal and natural responses so you'll know that your reactions are not crazy or abnormal. For those of you who are concerned about someone else's well-being, it's equally valuable to know the range of normal reactions so you don't accidentally plant false ideas that could misguide or even hurt the person you care about.

Here are some helpful explanations about the eight most common reactions to the death of someone important to you.

Numbness

A sense of numbness is the most common reaction you're likely to experience in the days and weeks immediately following the death of someone meaningful in your life. It's the body's way of protecting you from the amount and intensity of feeling caused by the death. Please understand that numbness is a normal—and even healthy—protection from the sometimes-overwhelming impact of a death. We often refer to the numbness as "emotional Novocain." Even though numbness is a normal and typical reaction, not knowing that's true sometimes causes grievers to think there's something wrong with them or that they are crazy. Nothing could be further from the truth.

Numbness for the Griever Tends to Occur Whether the Death Was Sudden or Was the Result of a Long-Term Illness— and a Few Words about "Shock"

In extremely rare situations, people go into a full-fledged medical reaction known as shock. Shock can be a major medical emergency: "A generally temporary massive physiological reaction to severe physical or emotional trauma, usually characterized by marked loss of blood pressure and depression of vital processes."

Shock generally only happens when there's been a sudden and/or violent death. As the definition explains, shock is usually a temporary condition and is quite different from the numbness described above which can last for weeks or months, or even longer.

It's also important to note that receiving the shocking news of a sudden, unexpected death doesn't typically thrust someone into a medical state of shock. Shock is one of the words that is sometimes misused and creates confusion between the general sense of being caught totally off guard by the news of a death and the serious medical condition called shock.

Reduced Ability to Concentrate or Focus

After the initial numbness wears off, most people continue to experience difficulty concentrating or focusing even on the simplest of tasks. Of all the normal reactions, this is the most universal one and affects the largest amount of grieving people. It's very common for grievers to be in one room, decide to go into another to do something and, when they get there, not have a clue what they're doing there. Please don't be surprised when and if that happens. It is totally normal in the circumstances.

The length of time the difficulty concentrating lasts is different for everyone so we can't give you an exact time frame. For some people, it's days or weeks, for others, months. We can tell you that the length of time the reduced ability to concentrate persists relates to many factors. One is the individual personality of the griever. Another is the degree to which a grieving person is able to discover and complete what was left emotionally unfinished by the death.

The actions of grief recovery can help you distinguish between the "raw grief" that is your normal and natural reaction to the death and the equally normal "unresolved grief" that relates to the unfinished emotions that are part of the physical ending of all relationships. One last note about concentration: You may notice that reading is difficult. You might find yourself reading the same paragraph over and over. If that happens, please know that it's well within the range of normal and natural, and that it's okay to put the book down for a while.

Crying or NOT Crying

Crying is obviously a normal reaction to the death of someone important to you. But even though you may find yourself crying a lot, you may also notice there are times that your tears have dried up and that you don't seem to feel much at all. If and when that happens, please don't be alarmed. Some people think if they stop crying, even for a short time, it somehow means they didn't love the person who died. That's not true. Emotions are exhausting and sometimes your heart and your body need to take a break.

Some people don't cry at all and become very concerned that there's something wrong with them because they haven't cried—as if they somehow didn't love or care about the person who died. That's not true either. It's usually an aspect of numbness. It is also the possible by-product of a life-long habit of pushing sad feelings down or away because of the fear of being judged for crying.

Lowered State of Energy—Not To Be Confused with Clinical Depression

The largest problem facing grievers is the incorrect use of the word "depressed" or "depression" to explain how they feel. The problem is that, in clinical terms, depression means something different than it does in relation to grief.

The best way to understand the difference is to use the most practical definition of depress, which is to push down, like "depress the gas pedal." The fact is that grief is a pushing down of energy, both emotional and physical. Grief can be all-consuming and robs energy. Describing how you feel as a lowered state of energy, instead of depression, helps remove the incorrect idea that you are clinically depressed when it is grief that is dominating your heart, mind, and body. (Caution: If you think you might be outside the range of normal grief, please contact a psychiatrist or therapist in your community.)

Disturbed Sleeping Patterns

Many people report major upheavals in their sleeping habits and patterns following the death of someone important to them. Obviously, those who lived with the person who died are most affected since the other person was a constant part of their daily life. That's not to say you might not be so affected if you lived far away from someone you loved. We know we repeat these words a lot, but it's "normal and natural" for many of your routines to be disrupted, and sleep is probably the most common one. When the activities of the day have ended and it's quiet—and often you're alone—sleep doesn't always come easily. And when it does come, it isn't always restful.

Dreams and Nightmares

Some people report an abundance of dreams, while others are concerned that they're not remembering any dreams when ordinarily they do. Still others tell us of nightmares involving the person who died. Although these reactions can be frightening and uncomfortable, they nevertheless are well within the range of normal. Some people cannot seem to sleep at all, while others can't seem to get out of bed. And some find themselves going back and forth between those extremes. Yes, it is uncomfortable and even a bit scary but, for most people, as they adapt to the absence of the other person, their sleeping habits return to their personal norms.

Irregular Eating Patterns

To repeat, grief brings a disruption in many of our normal routines. As with the extremes in sleep, some people just aren't interested in food at all, while others can't stop eating. And many go back and forth between the two. Even though it's normal and natural, it can really be confusing. Again, for most people, as they adapt to the absence of the other person, their eating patterns will return to their personal norms. With both sleeping and eating, you need to be patient with yourself and not try to hurry yourself back to your old routines. Just be careful with both issues from a health point of view and if things get out of hand for an extended period of time, see a doctor or a mental health professional.

Roller Coaster of Emotions

In the days, weeks, and months following the death of someone important, grievers often find themselves on an emotional roller coaster ride like no other experience they've ever had. A constant review of the relationship with the person who died is playing 24/7 in their minds and hearts. They may or may not be consciously aware of it, but it is happening. In fact, it is one of the reasons that concentration and focus are so difficult for grieving people.

Since the review accesses all aspects of the relationship—the good and the not-so-good, and in some cases the really bad— every possible emotion is triggered. Grievers can go from inconsolably sad with the awareness that their loved one is gone, to fond memories of happy times that bring smiles to their faces. This too is well within the range of normal and natural reactions.

As with the other things we've listed here, if or when you notice any of them happening, please be gentle with yourself. And if something seems troubling to you or beyond what you believe may be normal, please contact a mental health professional in your community.

Each of us is unique and every relationship is unique. Each of us experiences the upheaval of grief individually, including the degree to which we are affected by some or all of the common reactions outlined above.

Don't let anyone define your grief for you. There are no stages of grief and there are no time lines that can accurately define all grievers.

Stuck on a Painful Image

The issue of a recurring, painful last image or images of someone important to us who has died is sadly common for many grieving people. Whether the image pops up during sleep in dreams or nightmares, or while we are awake as the result of any number of reminders of the person who died, it can be tremendously upsetting. In addition to the pain they cause, those images often make us afraid to think about and remember the person we loved because it seems as if the only thing we can think of is that last terrible image.

Another aspect of the image problem is that for many people, the only image they are remembering is that last horrible one at the end of their person's life and the thousands of other images from a lifetime with that person seem to go out of focus or even disappear. As you probably already know, any attempt to try "not to think about it" doesn't work. The fact is some of those last images are really powerful and in a manner of speaking, it seems as if they are burned into your brain.

Over the years, to help people whose lives were dominated and limited by those kinds of images, we developed a way to help them have the painful images recede into the background and take their place within the entire relationship with the person who died, instead of being the only images they remember. On pages 157 and 158 of *The Grief Recovery Handbook* is a heading titled, "Stuck on a Painful Image." We have reprinted it for you below so you can get immediate benefit from the guidance it contains. In the meantime, we also suggest you get a copy of *The Grief Recovery Handbook* and read it and take all the actions it suggests.

Stuck on a Painful Image

From pages 157–158 of *The Grief Recovery Handbook* (Copyright © 1998, John W. James, Russell Friedman, HarperCollins Publishers):

One of the most painful of all experiences is to have a loved one die violently. You may have seen the accident or the aftermath. You may have seen photos of the scene. Or you may only have the pictures your imagination has conjured up. In any event, for many people, the imagery seems constant, as if it will never cease. Some of you may have equally disturbing images of your loved one's final hours, days, or weeks as they struggled through a terminal illness. The devastating nature of some diseases often alters appearance so much that you hardly recognize someone you have known your entire life.

Most people, in trying to help a friend, will tell them not to think about it. That is very nearly impossible. We think it is more helpful to acknowledge that the images and pictures are indeed horrible and painful. We also believe that the griever needs to be gently reminded that they have many thousands of other images as well.

We do not all get to go "gently into that good night" as poetry would have it. A woman tells us of her husband's final night at the hospital, with vivid details. Our response is, "What a horrible final picture that is for you." Then we ask, "Do you remember the first time you saw the man who became your husband?" She says yes, and we say, "Tell us what he looked like that day." And she does.

We all have tens of thousands of images of our loved ones. Some of the images are wonderful and happy. Some are negative and sad. And sometimes the final ones are very painful, as when violence or disease have altered how someone looked. It is unrealistic to tell someone not to remember what they saw or imagined. By acknowledging the discomfort of the final, unpleasant pictures, we allow the remembering of all the other pictures. Each time the ending pictures crop up, they must be acknowledged.

Acknowledging the painful pictures and remembering others does not deny or minimize the painful ones. When grievers are allowed and encouraged to state what they are experiencing, the painful pictures subside more quickly. This leaves more room for the review of the entire relationship, not just the ending.

ABOUT THE AUTHORS

Russell Friedman and **John W. James** are the authors of the bestselling *Grief Recovery Handbook* and *When Children Grieve*. Together they run the Grief Recovery Institute, www.grief recoverymethod.com. Both authors live in Los Angeles.